Lester Raymer

A Collection
of Essays

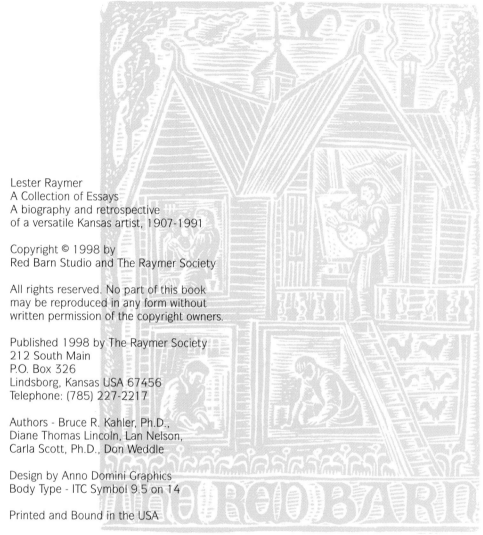

Lester Raymer
A Collection of Essays
A biography and retrospective
of a versatile Kansas artist, 1907-1991

Published 1998 by The Raymer Society
212 South Main
P.O. Box 326
Lindsborg, Kansas USA 67456
Telephone: (785) 227-2217

Authors - Bruce R. Kahler, Ph.D.,
Diane Thomas Lincoln, Lan Nelson,
Carla Scott, Ph.D., Don Weddle

Design by Anno Domini Graphics
Body Type - ITC Symbol 9.5 on 14

Printed and Bound in the USA

ISBN 0-9667032-0-0

Library of Congress 98-067733

*Cover: Untitled, drummer boy,
oil on board, 1962,
Raymer Society collection, gift from
Barbara and Roger Ellis.
Photo by
Jaderborg photography.*

*This page: "The Red Barn"
promotional card,
actual size, woodcut, 1949.*

*Opposite Page:
Chanticleer, wire, nd,
Birger Sandzén Memorial Gallery,
Greenough Trust Collection.*

Lester Raymer
A Collection of Essays

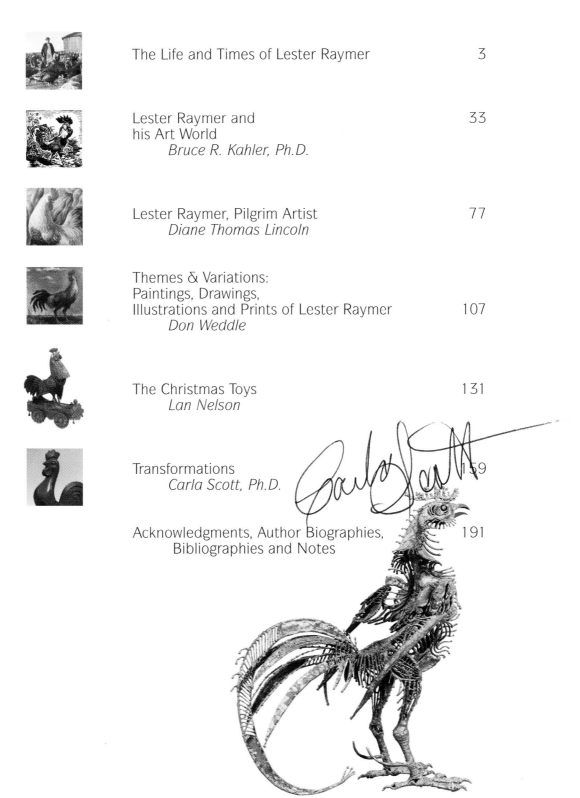

Lester Raymer

. . . born in Oklahoma, educated at the School of the Art Institute of Chicago, created his first art studio in Oklahoma after college, married Ramona Weddle and settled in Lindsborg, Kansas. There, he created The Red Barn Studio. He was a quiet man, outspoken through his artwork. This image of Lester Raymer (81), and one of his harlequins, was taken at the Red Barn Studio in 1988.

Photo by
Jaderborg Photography.

Introduction

The author of each essay in this book seeks to inform the readers about Lester Raymer's environment and the influences in his life. Raymer's role as an artist within the context of the artistic community of Lindsborg, Kansas, is presented by Bruce R. Kahler, a professor of History and Art History at Bethany College in Lindsborg. Don Weddle, artist and retired art teacher, focuses on the primary passions of Raymer: painting, watercolor, drawing, illustration and printmaking. Christian symbolism and biblical representations permeate Raymer's artwork in the media he explored. Diane Thomas Lincoln, artist and professor of art in Wichita, Kansas, explores Raymer's spiritual visions.

Lester Raymer married Ramona Weddle in 1945 and began a tradition of creating a gift of love for her each year at Christmas. Beginning in 1960, these gifts focused on toys patterned after traditional and antique toys. Lan Nelson, artist and special friend of the Raymers, presents the thematic and chronological development of these toys. Dr. Carla Scott, artist and Executive Director of the Raymer Society, focuses on the transformations Raymer made to enhance the aesthetic of the Red Barn Studio, the "potboilers" created to produce income in the early days, and the three-dimensional artwork he created.

The essays were developed independently, yet the writing team met regularly to maintain a focus and uniformity of presentation. The writers' exploration of a topic may overlap information from other essays where it is necessary to support concepts. The introductory biographical information is a compilation of information from combined research. In addition, Sally Johnson, artist and member of the staff at the Red Barn Studio, interviewed visitors who knew the Raymers. She spent many hours reviewing text for this book.

Information about Lester Raymer, his life and his art, continues to be revealed. The writers recognize that this is not a comprehensive nor conclusive text about Raymer; rather it is the 'Beginnings.'

The Life and Times of Lester Raymer

Above: Raymer Family Surrey.

Top, this page: Entrance door to Red Barn Studio, photo by Jim Richardson.

Facing page: Raymer Family Portrait. Parents: John C. and Carrie (Erb) Raymer. Boys, left to right: Lester, Harold, John A. Photos furnished by John and Jan Raymer.

THE EARLY YEARS

Raymer's father, John C. Raymer, and his mother, Carrie (Erb), farmed near Naperville, Illinois. Here they had their first child, a daughter, who died as an infant. Carrie and John both grew up in families that were of Pennsylvania Dutch descent. Although John learned English, Carrie spoke German and broken English all her life. Soon after their marriage in 1902, John decided they should join other family members who had moved to Oklahoma homestead territory. Once John located a homestead a few miles west of what is now Alva, Oklahoma, he sent word for Carrie to join him. Carrie, accustomed to her city surroundings and fine things for the home, brought her fine crystal, china, special household items, a collection of books, and her pump organ. The Raymers were the first in the community to have a surrey when everyone else had wagons to drive and, later, the first to own a car.

It was in Oklahoma that Raymer and his two brothers, Harold and John, were born and reared. John Archibald Raymer was born in 1905, Lester Wilton Raymer was born September 24, 1907, and Harold Grantham Raymer was born in 1911.

3

Left: Carrie Raymer

Center: John C. Raymer
Oil on canvas,
by Lester Raymer, ca 1935,
private collection.

Right: Harold, Lester, and John
A. Raymer, ca 1917.

In his childhood, Lester Raymer chose to do chores inside the house to help his mother rather than helping with the outdoor farm work. He learned to cook the Amish type foods which were common in the Raymer household. One of his special skills in cooking, which he perfected as an adult, was his ability to prepare superb curried fried rabbit. Sewing, quilting, and needlework were skills Raymer learned from his mother at an early age. He watched how his mother transformed scraps of fabric into beautiful quilts. Impressed with the ways his father was able to transform ordinary objects into useful things for family and friends, Raymer said that his father could do just about anything, "He even fixed the soles on our shoes." The resourcefulness of his parents modeled for Raymer an ability to see beauty and soul in what others discarded.

Neighbor Fred Taylor, Sr.'s barn was full of everything. When someone needed something, which seemingly did not exist, Taylor would say, "Let me see now," then go find exactly what was needed. Being around the Taylor farm, Raymer developed his passion for collecting, what seemed to many, worthless stuff. The Raymer farm had a small forge which John C. Raymer utilized. But the Taylor's barn housed a better forge. As a child, Lester Raymer learned from both men how to transform scrap metal into something useful.

Carrie Raymer belonged to the Church of the Brethren located about two miles from the Raymer farmstead. She had her pump organ moved to the church so that she could provide music for worship. Later she became a member of the Wesley Methodist church in Alva where a Raymer relative was preaching. Every night Carrie would read to the family from the large, illustrated family Bible. The pictures in that Bible became a rich source of images for Raymer. Carrie's sister, Susie, married the Reverend Ira Jacob Sollenberger who was a Church of the Brethren preacher. From a very early

A Raymer family outing.

age Raymer and his Uncle Sollenberger talked about theology, spirituality, and, in later years, a little politics.

As Lester's father's health declined, the rest of the family was required to take on more of the farm chores. This included working the fields with a team of horses pulling a plow. A clear image remained in Raymer's mind of the day the circus train of horses and elephants passed by their farm. It is believed the smell of the elephants spooked the plow horses. The team took out on a dead run pulling Carrie behind them and overturning the plow. Raymer and his brothers finally managed to get the horses stopped.

Doctors suggested to John C. Raymer that a move to a drier climate might help his tuberculosis, so the Raymer family decided to move to Colorado. They first traveled to Naperville, Illinois, to visit family. Then the Sollenbergers and Raymers traveled together cross-country from Illinois to Colorado. For the overnight rests on the journey, the two cars were parked back to back and a tent set up between them. The Raymers and Sollenbergers settled in Aurora, Colorado, less than five blocks from one another. At this time, Lester was in the seventh or eighth grade.

The Raymer's family made regular visits back to the Elgin and Naperville, Illinois, area to visit relatives. Several members of Carrie's family, the Erbs, worked at the Marshall Fields department store located near the School of the Art Institute of Chicago. During these family visits, Raymer decided that he would attend the Art Institute upon graduation from high school. Several years after high school, Raymer had earned enough money for tuition to enter the school, provided he stay with relatives in the Chicago area. While at the Art Institute, Raymer met Ramona Weddle.

Ramona and friends,
Estes Park, Colo., 1931.

Ramona on a train,
Chicago, 1930.

"Wrapping paper for
gifts to Madam,"
one of Ramona's design projects,
Raymer Society Archives.

RAMONA

Ramona Weddle was born October 17, 1909 at the Brunswick Hotel in Lindsborg, Kansas. Her parents, Ed and Cora (Shields) Weddle were owners of the Brunswick. The Hotel was built in 1886 at a cost of $22,000. When hard times came, the hotel was converted into a college dorm. In 1897 Ed Weddle's father bought the Brunswick for Cora and Ed, to help them get started in life together. Ed and Cora Weddle owned the Brunswick until 1946. Ramona Weddle loved to talk about her memories of growing up in the Brunswick and sharing her home with the hotel visitors. She especially remembered the sample room with the wide exterior doors to accommodate the sample trunks of the visiting salesman. Some of the salesmen would bring as many as 20 trunks of samples. The salesmen were met at the train station by Brunswick staff with a horse and wagon. The carriage barn was just south of the hotel. The salesmen would bring special candy for Ramona, her brother and her sister. Many of the samples not sold, especially anything broken, were left in the sample room. She often commented that she probably had the best collection of broken dolls. Eventually some of these dolls became models for Raymer's paintings and provided parts for the assemblages and toys he created.

Ramona began her college career at Bethany College in Lindsborg, then transferred to Kansas State College in Manhattan, Kansas. She was named to the Delta Phi Delta national arts fraternity as a student at Kansas State. She transferred to the School of the Art Institute of Chicago in the fall of 1930. Ramona Weddle and Lester Raymer became a part of a small group of students who regularly shared time together.

After college, Weddle did not pursue her own creative art making except on rare occasions. When she left the Art Institute, Weddle continued to work in Chicago until 1940 or 1941. At that time, she moved back to Lindsborg to help her parents with the hotel business. During World War II, there was a shortage of professors at Bethany College so Ramona agreed to teach the women's physical education classes. She and her physical education students toured the gardens of Lindsborg for their exercise.

6

Agnes and Ramona,
Zion City, Illinois, 1937.

Lester, Ramona (right),
and friends at "Mary
Chamber's house in Oakpark,"
Illinois, 1931.

"Backdrop for Adagio Dance,"
stage design, "Persian motif,"
Ramona Weddle,
Raymer Society Collection.

Untitled, rooster,
oil on canvas, 1944
Birger Sandzén
Memorial Gallery,
Greenough Trust Collection.

Mom (Carrie) Raymer with
Lester's nephew John in the
turkey pen. Okla.

CHICAGO TO ALVA

In the fall of 1933 Raymer's parents came to visit him in Chicago. Soon after they arrived, his father died. Raymer decided to drop out of college and return to Oklahoma with his mother. They moved in with Lester's brother, John A. Raymer and his wife, Edna, who had moved back to the Raymer farm in 1930. For many years, Carrie Raymer maintained the home in Aurora, Colorado, as a rental home.

For two years after John C. Raymer died, Edna Raymer remembers that Carrie Raymer cried what seemed like most of the time. Her mood finally changed when John and Edna Raymer's son, Johnnie (John), was born in 1935. Carrie Raymer spent many hours caring for this grandson which led to a lifelong bond. John and Edna Raymer's younger son, Ellis, was born in 1941.

When Raymer left the Art Institute, he was classified as a senior. He completed his academic courses at Northwestern University in Alva. The Art Institute granted Raymer a diploma in 1935 and a bachelor's degree was

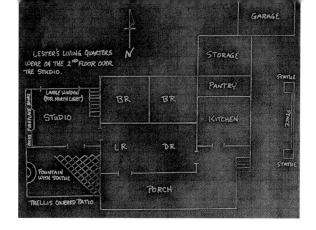

Floorplan of house/studio in
Oklahoma,
courtesy John Raymer.

conferred by the Art Institute in May, 1946. Although there are no records
of the courses he taught, Alva residents remember Raymer teaching painting
and drawing for a summer term as an adjunct faculty member at
Northwestern. At that time, the university kept the regular faculty names
listed with the class, even if an adjunct was actually teaching.

Raymer's first art studio was created from the abandoned home located
on an additional farm his parents owned. Raymer and his family dismantled the
old house, rebuilt it and attached it to the southwest corner of the family farm
house. The second story became his living quarters and the main level his
studio. He created a courtyard area with a pole fence much like those he had
seen in the Southwest. He planted vines to grow on the fence and over the
arbor area. At the same time, Raymer changed the rather plain farm yard into
a garden, including cacti from New Mexico and a forest of shrubs. Raymer
utilized this studio for eleven years, from 1934 to 1945. As John Raymer grew
up during this time, he was fascinated with Uncle Lester's art and the studio.

During this period, Raymer produced artwork on a regular basis.
Subject matter for his paintings and watercolors included roosters, religious
imagery, horses, still life work incorporating flowers or fruit, scenes of clowns
and the circus, and close-up landscapes of hills or driftwood. He also
produced several illustrations, thinking he might get work as an illustrator.
Raymer would go out to herd turkeys, sketch book in hand. When the turkeys
were grazing, Raymer would sketch for hours. He never really helped with the
family farm work, except during planting and harvest seasons. He would
sleep during the day or herd the turkeys and do his artwork at night. He was,
however, very helpful with household work and the cooking.

Although the primary focus of his art was painting and drawing, Raymer's
tradition of working in a variety of media began here in Oklahoma. Materials for
artwork included found objects, scrap materials, and "junk". Raymer's passion
for farm auctions and sales proved to be a major source for these materials. The
prairie environment was another major source of materials. John enjoyed following his uncle through the pastures picking up animal horns and old wood.
Sometimes they would do a little rabbit hunting for the evening meal.

Being close to Fred Taylor, their neighbor, allowed Raymer to perfect
his skills in blacksmithing. Scrap metal, old farm tools and equipment, and
other objects were transformed into artwork. He used Taylor's blacksmith
equipment and discussed ideas with him. Raymer created a number of metal

Dinner at the Raymers home.
From L to R - Gladys Steck,
(Naperville,) Grandma Currie,
Edna Raymer, John A. Raymer,
Lester Raymer, ca 1944.

9

Lester in front of Raymer
farmstead in Oklahoma,
ca 1930.

sculptures and ironwork for fences, gates and other exterior locations during this time. It was typical for farm homes to have no electricity during the 1930s and the Raymer farm was no exception. To provide light, Raymer fashioned junk (broken parts of old metal objects including pieces of farm equipment) into candle holders and hanging candle fixtures for his living space and studio. The green hanging candle fixture in the Red Barn Studio is one Raymer made in Oklahoma.

The courtyard Raymer designed was right outside his studio. This space was used for creating sculptures, sand casting with concrete, welding, and wood carving. Some of the sand cast sculptures were transported by Raymer when he moved to the Red Barn Studio and placed in a brick fence between the front garage and the north entrance. Sculptures of a cherub and a fish, created in Oklahoma, are now in the north room of the Red Barn Studio.

Wood sculptures carved by Raymer while in Oklahoma include a Madonna and Child, a large horse head, and a small red rooster. Walks through the pasture and trips back to Colorado to visit relatives were the two main sources for his wood. Raymer used cottonwood and aspen roots when possible as both are soft woods.

Raymer created a red rooster for the entrance to the courtyard. The rooster had no base as the legs simply fit into the fence. A base was added when it was moved to the Red Barn Studio. Raymer used a hatchet to begin carving on a big block of wood. Smaller tools were used to fine-tune details. The horse head and the Madonna and Child sculptures are now in the Red Barn Studio in Lindsborg.

Mrs. Marjorie Sawyer-Munson, owner of the Munson Hatchery in Alva, became a patron of Raymer's work. Many years after Raymer had moved to Lindsborg, Alva women, including Mrs. Munson, made trips to the Red Barn Studio to have Raymer sign the early Raymer artwork they owned. They also continued to purchase work from him at the Red Barn Studio. People from Oklahoma were regular customers into the 1980s. In 1985, a small group of people representing the Alva Centennial committee came from Alva, to ask Raymer to identify a painting of the Alva Courthouse. They thought Raymer completed the painting while he was still in Oklahoma. Raymer said he was almost sure it was his painting. The Centennial committee asked for permission to use the image on commercially printed note cards and posters to help raise support for the Alva Centennial celebration.

Antique flintlock with gun stock carved by Lester Raymer, ca 1937, Red Barn Studio. Photo by Jim Richardson.

At Oklahoma farm sales Raymer purchased antique muzzle loading guns, some dating back to pre-Civil War times. He carved elaborate imagery on the stocks or created new stocks with his own images. The metal work of the guns was often altered and sometimes completely changed. Raymer used the animal horns he found in the pasture to create powder horns, carving designs on the surface. He took apart musical instruments, collected from farm sales, and altered the metal to serve as tips and caps for the powder horns. Raymer made shot for these guns by dropping molten lead from the windmill tower into a tub of cold water. The lead would form into a sphere as it fell through the air and solidify when it hit the water. The guns and powder horns were moved to the Red Barn Studio.

Powder horn by Lester Raymer, ca 1937, Red Barn Studio.

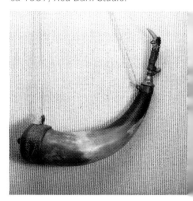

Watercolor drawing, circus horses, acrobats, ca 1940, Raymer Society Collection.

Wood carving of horse head, ca 1937, Red Barn Studio.

Raymer followed the circus and wild west shows from town to town during the 1930s and early 1940s. Sometimes he would walk the elephants for the circus. He spent a great deal of time sketching while at the circus shows. Circus imagery created by Raymer while in Oklahoma depicted clowns, horses with circus tents in the background, and circus scenes with performers. Many of these were watercolors. He also made masks of circus clowns using papier maché techniques. These masks decorated the studio wall next to the stairs going up to Raymer's living quarters.

Raymer was fascinated with horses. As a child, he loved to watch his parents' team of horses work the fields. The Raymers had two fine teams of horses: one for work and the other to pull the family buggy. In his adult years, Raymer's brother, Harold, raised rodeo stunt horses and his brother, John, used horses in the farm work and cattle roundups. Horses were a major part of the circus and wild west shows which Raymer visited in Oklahoma and later in Kansas. Fred Taylor was also an excellent horseman. Raymer's watercolors completed in the early 1940s included circus horses or a plain background with a number of horses as dominant images. This interest in horses is also evident in his later work, especially in the sculptures and toys he created at the Red Barn Studio.

12

Lester and Ramona,
Wedding Day,
October 12, 1945.

To Lindsborg

From 1933 to 1945 relatives recall that Lester Raymer received mail from Lindsborg, and travelled there occasionally. Friends and family of Ramona Weddle remember that Raymer assisted her with painting windows for the Lindsborg festivals in the early 1940s. They also recall that Ed and Cora Weddle provided a room for Lester and hired him to assist Ramona with the management of the Brunswick while they went to Chicago for Christmas during the early 1940s.

At that time, Raymer used a corner of the Brunswick dining room as studio space. Several people from Lindsborg commissioned portraits between 1942 and 1944. They sat for these portraits at the Brunswick. Raymer and Weddle spent time with Margaret Sandzén Greenough and Royer and Althea Barclay on a regular basis beginning in 1942. Margaret Greenough and Althea Barclay were among many of Ramona's special life-long friends. The Barclays recall that Raymer and Weddle spent Christmas Eves with them beginning in the early 1940s. Ramona said that during one of Lester's Christmas visits they decided to marry at a future date.

Raymer's presence in Lindsborg beginning in the early 1940s suggests he was aware that Birger Sandzén, professor of art at Bethany College was nearing retirement and that the college would likely be searching for a new art professor.

In 1946, the Raymer families relocated on farms near Burlington, Kansas, where relatives were already living. Carrie Raymer lived with Harold and his wife, Maxine, while John and Edna lived in a farm not far from them. The Oklahoma farm was again rented out.

Wedding party, (from l to r)
Preacher's wife, Preacher,
Ramona, Lester, Cora and Ed
Weddle. Lindsborg, Kansas.

13

*Red Barn Studio,
interior display, ca 1950.*

*Untitled, ceramic horse
sculpture, Jean Wolshagel,
with Lester Raymer,
private collection.*

Ramona Weddle and Lester Raymer married on October 12, 1945, at 10 a.m. in Lindsborg, Kansas. The wedding was held in Ramona's church, the Messiah Lutheran Church. They went to Taos, New Mexico, on their honeymoon. Upon their return to Lindsborg, they set up house in a room at the Brunswick. Lester continued to use his art studio in the Brunswick. He created gallery space in the public areas to display his artwork. He made several trips back to Oklahoma for his belongings. The Barclays lent their farm truck for these moves and later, to move things to and from Taos. Raymer used the truck to move sculptures, paintings, metal work, prints, guns, art supplies, the forge, the book press, and furniture.

Ramona's parents gave the newlyweds the laundry building and carriage barn once utilized by the Brunswick. These buildings were located on the property south of the hotel, at the west end of the lot. The Weddles purchased the white house on the front part of this property as their retirement home. Lester and Ramona Raymer renovated the laundry building as their first home. The carriage barn was renovated for Raymer's art studio.

In 1946-47, Raymer taught art at Bethany College. During that time, many of his students were men returning home from the war. The GI bill helped support their college studies. Among these students were Milford Greer, Bob Walker and Don Weddle. These students and many other individuals in the community, became significant friends of the Raymers. Bob Walker and his first wife, Mariella, visited the Raymers frequently until they moved to California where Bob continued his studies. Walker wrote to the Raymers in 1948, "How homesick we sometimes feel for those incomparable evenings at the Raymers when we listened to symphonies, talked music, art, and Bethany College." When they moved back to Lindsborg in the early 1970s, the Walkers became Sunday tea time regulars at the Raymers. After Walker's first wife died, he married Rita Sharpe, and the tea time tradition continued for many years.

After completing his degree at the School of the Art Institute of Chicago, Don Weddle taught art in Wichita, Kansas, and pursued his own artwork. He kept in touch with the Raymers through the student field trips he scheduled to the Red Barn Studio and visits home to see his family and friends. In later years, Weddle established his art studio in Lindsborg. He was instrumental in formulating the Raymer Society (explained in later text) and organizing the 1988 Raymer Retrospective at the Birger Sandzén Memorial

Easel with Lester Raymer's last painting Red Barn Studio. Photo by Jim Richardson, 1998.

Art Gallery in Lindsborg, Kansas. In addition to press releases about Raymer and the exhibition, Weddle wrote an article about Raymer and the Red Barn Studio which was published in *Southwest Art* in 1988.

As an artist in Lindsborg, Raymer had many friends, especially among the artistic community. They recognized the quiet artist as a mentor, friend, and someone with whom they could share artistic visions. These friends were often special friends of Ramona as well. Raymer enjoyed sharing his life with friends who had left Lindsborg through letters. The letters were full of illustrations of artwork in progress, information about books and movies, revelations of how the music he was listening to caused his "soul to sing," requests for information about materials for his artwork, and, sometimes, even conversations about politics.

Raymer was not a person to share his studio or artistic visions openly and freely. He was very quiet, outspoken only when he thought the individual was sincere. He was also outspoken when the conversations turned to one on one discussions about art and religion. Sharing, however, was important to Raymer. He enjoyed sharing new ideas with working artists and art professors.

For Raymer there was a special joy in mentoring beginning artists. Brandon Sherwood, an artist working with wood, began his artistic career partially as a result of many discussions with Raymer. Sherwood currently lives in Salina, Kansas. Raymer would send books home with him to read and then discuss the ideas on his return visits. Lan Nelson and Julie Unruh, artists now living in Lindsborg, learned the art of tin star making from Raymer. Beth Walker, daughter of Bob Walker, remembers Raymer taking time to help her understand her own artistic longings and ideas.

Jean Wolshagel from Lyons, Kansas, worked in the studio two to three days a week to fulfill requirements for an independent study sculpture class she was completing with Professor Rosemary Laughflin at Bethany College in 1956-57. Raymer wrote, "If you look real sharp you can dimly see some of the sand molded concrete sculpture reliefs that I and Jeannie did. I so enjoyed having her working in the studio."

George Boles, a Bethany College alum who studied art, became a friend and studio assistant during the 1950s. Boles assisted Raymer with many aspects of clay production and mosaic work.

John Whitfield, an artist living in Lindsborg, shared Raymer's passion for creating art. He became a friend the Raymers felt comfortable to call when they needed help as their health deteriorated. Throughout the years art professors visited the Red Barn to share professional ideas with Raymer. Artists Mark and Mardel Esping shared many hours talking about art with Raymer. They became a source for materials and ideas as well as individuals who promoted Raymer's work through the galleries they owned in Lindsborg.

Perhaps the most artistic sharing on a day-to-day basis beginning in the early days of the Red Barn Studio was between Raymer and Malcolm Esping. Esping was an artist in Lindsborg who worked with artistic blacksmithing and metal work. He used special techniques to make traditional Swedish wedding crowns. In the 1950s Esping had an art studio and gallery on West State Street just west of Main Street. In the late 1960s Esping moved his studio, the Sloyd to south Main Street, less than a block north of the Red Barn studio. Although Raymer visited the Sloyd regularly, most of the business between the two happened as they walked past one another on the street. A mutual friend, Leo Opat, says, "They would stop to converse about a solution to a problem or an idea for a project, but mostly they would just 'cuss and discuss.'"

Esping created the mosaic in the sidewalk in front of Bethany Lutheran Church in Lindsborg as well as a number of other liturgical commissions for churches in the region. He made porch railings, special crosses commemorating weddings, jewelry of all types and, occasionally, assisted Raymer with projects. Esping was the mastermind behind solutions to how mechanisms could be designed for the toys Raymer made for his wife. Although Raymer had a forge, he utilized his friend's shop frequently. Not only was Esping's equipment far superior, he was available for advice. Raymer wrote to Greer, "I spend mornings at Malcolm's shop working with his equipment." And later he wrote, "Finished hand forged hinges for garage doors in Taos. I have been using Malcolm Esping's shop to do quite a bit of the iron work that will be used in the Taos house. Plan on a lot more." The two men also shared one another's studios as "hideouts" when tour buses were in town.

Malcom with onlookers at Art in the Park, Lindsborg, Kansas.

The Raymers had many other friends with whom they shared time and artistic work. Some of these friendships developed with students at Bethany, others were individuals who visited the studio on field trips, while others were artists living in the region. Both Lester and Ramona Raymer had friends not directly involved in the arts. Some individuals became friends as they shared their "junk treasures."

Dale Hoag knew Raymer for almost fifty years. Hoag was a photographer in Lindsborg and then became a building contractor. In 1980, Hoag opened the Könstverk Gallery in Lindsborg representing many area artists including Raymer. By this time, Raymer's failing health had all but halted his artwork. Shortly after opening the Könstverk, Hoag talked Raymer into booking a watercolor exhibition for the Könstverk in 1982. He bought

Untitled, Taos studio.
Watercolor sketch,
Milford Greer, 1960,
Raymer Society Archives.

Untitled,
view from Taos property.
Watercolor sketch,
Milford Greer, 1960,
Raymer Society Archives.

Raymer the finest watercolors and gave him scraps of archival mat board. "I am proud to have started Raymer working again," said Hoag.

"He really started by doing a few crayon drawings, then the watercolor, and that got him started doing more with his paintings again." Hoag was the person who initiated the process of electing Raymer for the Kansas Governor's Artist Award in 1984, and, in the late 1980s, advised the Raymers about establishing the Raymer Society.

Larry Smith, a musician, corresponded with Raymer for over twenty years. He was actively involved in the changes made to the Red Barn Studio in the 1980s.

Milford Greer and Lester Raymer became lifelong friends. Raymer and Greer corresponded from the late 1940s until Greer's death in 1972. During the summer of 1947, Raymer and Greer were in Taos, New Mexico, for a summer graduate level art class. They spent the summer drawing and painting together in the countryside around Ranchos de Taos. Both artists produced numerous watercolors and sketches that summer. Raymer wrote to Greer in 1962 remembering this summer of 1947, "Do you remember the summer you and I spent in Taos and the first week we painted out west of town near the gravel quarry looking out across the stream to the southeast at an old two story house? I believe I painted my first landscape with this house."

While in Taos, they became familiar with the crafts movement in the area. Raymer and Greer decided to establish a craft studio in Lindsborg and hopefully, later, in Taos. Greer, by this time, was studying at the School of the Art Institute of Chicago. They planned that Raymer would begin the craft studio and Greer would be a part of it as often as he could. When Greer completed his studies he would join the studio full time. The Red Barn Craft Studio started when Raymer returned to Lindsborg in the fall of 1947.

Lester Raymer, ca 1960.

THE TAOS DREAM

One of Raymer's life dreams began in the late 1930s. His obsessive goal was to live in Taos, New Mexico. Before he ever moved to Lindsborg, Raymer tried to get his mother to move to Taos. She was not pleased with the environment or with being away from the rest of the family so the move was never made. By 1947, he and Greer began the Taos craft center dream which continued until Greer's untimely death in 1972. "How I wished we had that house in Taos," Raymer wrote to Greer in 1956, "...or someplace you could retire to and paint and keep vandals away when we weren't there. I would have a place of escape where I too perhaps could briefly get my head above the clouds to forget my feet of clay." Raymer says he is "dreaming of himself being able to own the property." By January of 1957, Raymer was a little closer to this dream. He had been to Taos to look at homes but everything was out of his price range.

Raymer's correspondence with Greer in the 1950s and 1960s expresses his passion to be in Taos, along with excuses about why he could not get there. "Taos will have to wait a bit but we will get there before too long I hope." Raymer was definitely planning to move to Taos. His letters include many references to furniture he was making for Taos, of metal work he was creating at Esping's studio for Taos, and of other things one might need for Taos.

Raymer traveled to Taos in the summer of 1959:

"Got home Tues. night. Went out to Taos this time with a made up mind that I wasn't going to get involved with realtors and real estate this time. Would look at the whole scene objectively, etc. But due to an

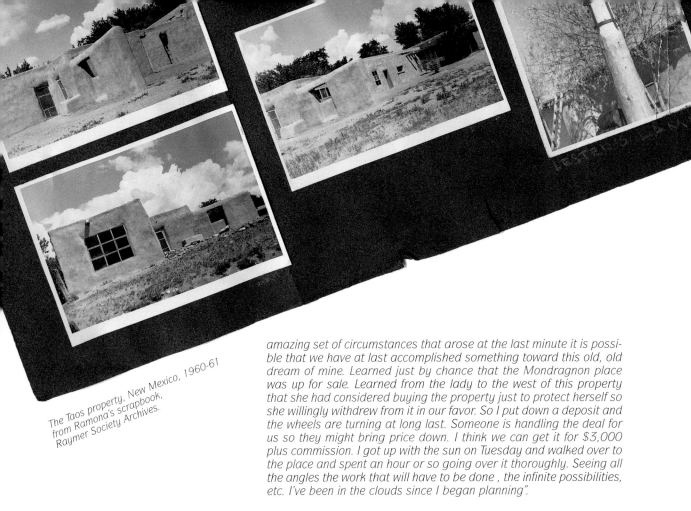

amazing set of circumstances that arose at the last minute it is possible that we have at last accomplished something toward this old, old dream of mine. Learned just by chance that the Mondragnon place was up for sale. Learned from the lady to the west of this property that she had considered buying the property just to protect herself so she willingly withdrew from it in our favor. So I put down a deposit and the wheels are turning at long last. Someone is handling the deal for us so they might bring price down. I think we can get it for $3,000 plus commission. I got up with the sun on Tuesday and walked over to the place and spent an hour or so going over it thoroughly. Seeing all the angles the work that will have to be done , the infinite possibilities, etc. I've been in the clouds since I began planning".

By July of 1960, Raymer and Greer had purchased a home in Ranchos De Taos, in close proximity to the well known Ranchos De Taos church. "I asked for possession by the first of August. I am working round the clock to get tiles ready to ship to Taos. Working now on a couple of things for the two religious shows that I've been invited to. Will come out as soon as I get them off." Raymer's next letter that summer says, "This project is on my mind every hour of every day and I actually dream of it. Hope to stay forever and a day. What will the area look like in the winter when all the trees are undressed?"

By August of 1960, Greer had moved from California to the Taos area. Raymer again asks Greer to send a list of things for him to bring to Taos and indicates that he is "thinking about a pickup truck." Royer Barclay lent the Raymers his farm truck regularly to take things to and from Taos. Raymer never did purchase his own truck. When he returned from Taos in August 1960, Raymer states, "It doesn't seem possible that only a week ago I was in Rancho de Taos." Later in the fall of 1960 Raymer writes, "Plan to leave Monday for Taos, appraisers here for estate Monday. Sent payment for house. Ramona will be traveling with me."

The letters Raymer wrote to Greer throughout the fall of 1960 are full of ideas for the remodeling of the Taos home. His attitude fluctuates between being "frustrated ...in Lindsborg when work is going on in Taos," to excitement about ideas for people who might help with the work of remodeling the Taos home. Raymer continues focusing his energies toward Taos so that by the spring of 1961 he says:

LESTER BY THE RIO GRANDE

New Mexico, 1960,
from Ramona's scrapbook.

"Been devoting about half my time to doors and such for the Taos home. Collecting spindles, windows and such. Found two salvage places in Hutchinson. Going back Wed. to pick up a door I found on the last trip. By begging and borrowing I am amassing a collection of doors, iron work, spindles, furniture and such that can be worked into the house. I spend mornings at Malcolm's shop working with his equipment. I'm fabricating a door at the moment out of one of the massive ones from the Swedish pavilion. Have it about ready for assembly and gluing of suitable hardware and iron work. Cleaning up and refinishing about a dozen odd chairs that I have collected, not Spanish but sufficiently interesting to bring."

Raymer was the partner who financed the house and Greer the partner who put most of the physical energies into the renovation of the home in Ranchos De Taos. Their dream ended soon, for by July 27, 1962, Raymer wrote, "ironic, all this scrambling for the money to buy a house that probably will be sold before I have a chance to ever use it. Plan to get away to Taos mid August." He concludes that selling the house is the only solution. Selling the house was not the end of Raymer's dream of being in Taos. On many occasions Raymer wrote Larry Smith about trips he and Ramona had made to Taos.

In later years, Raymer seemed to feel that it was the women in his life who prevented him from moving to Taos. First his mother and then Ramona. One opinion is that, in reality, Raymer's asthma and an allergic reaction to adobe was really the culprit. Some have speculated that it was simply an idea too late developed, that age seemed to prevent the move. Possibly, the challenge of setting up a house and an art school by two individuals leading separate lives was too great. There can only be conjecture as there is no conclusive evidence to support these theories.

The Taos property, New Mexico, 1960-61

Interior of Lester Raymer's
Red Barn Studio, 1998.
Photo by Jim Richardson.

THE RED BARN STUDIO

Although Raymer had already established a working space at the Brunswick Hotel in Lindsborg and was a producing artist, the Red Barn Craft Studio really began when Raymer returned from his 1947 summer in Taos. He had completed the renovation of the carriage house for the craft studio and was ready to begin a pottery production studio. This studio had walls and shelves for exhibition of work, a kiln, a potters' wheel, easels, and a table. Equipment such as the wedging table and the forge were kept outside until winter truly set in.

As the Red Barn Craft Studio evolved, it became a place filled with art and artifacts evoking spirits, signs to the soul. It takes one on a journey to many places through many art history periods. The studio was constantly evolving and changing throughout Raymer's life. Most of all, Raymer wanted to recreate an environment in his studio like those he had experienced in Mexico. Raymer traveled to Mexico and Taos several times between 1945 and 1965. These trips provided inspiration for the aesthetics of the studio environment and ideas for the craft production process. A wall of Mexican dishware and other small craft items from Mexico became an important part of the décor for The Red Barn Studio. The Mexican front door of the studio was fashioned by

Raymer using porch flooring to cover an old door. He created decorative nails, a metal sun face, a metal lion, and a knocker to embellish this door. On other studio doors, Raymer fashioned serpent-shaped knockers.

Raymer's letters to Milford Greer, and later to Larry Smith, chronicle the physical changes in the studio and the living quarters throughout the years. In November, 1948, Raymer writes that he is plastering bedrooms and seams in the wallboards to convert the laundry room into a home. The next spring Raymer says, "I have a yard to sow, a hedge to be planted between us and the Hotel, and a garden to be made." Raymer planted some of his favorite flowers, tulips, that spring. When they bloomed and faded in 1949 he lamented, "How sad it is to see all the gay colors of the tulips gone." By that spring the walls were nearly finished and Raymer had moved all the scrap lumber out of the way.

In the spring of 1956 Raymer writes, "...building a high brick wall enclosing a patio at the rear of the house. The wall will run from our garage over to the Red Barn. I plan to pave the patio with brick and maybe do a fountain for it. Part of it will be covered by an arbor on which there will be a wild grape vine. The patio will be a place to work in the hot summer, a place to sun bathe, and to relax." This project however, took a long time. In 1960, the patio wall was still only half done and Raymer was contemplating adding a Chinese smoke oven in the wall. "I am planting trees and shrubs and vines that will make it a delightful place to be in time." Raymer wrote to Smith in 1977, "The back patio wall is enclosed now." An idea conceived in 1956 was brought to conclusion in 1977.

This indicates that the Raymers were living in the renovated laundry room and that the converted barn was still serving as the Red Barn Studio as late as the spring of 1956. However, soon after the letter was written, the Raymers moved into the Weddle's home with Cora Weddle. Ed Weddle died in February of 1955. Cora Weddle maintained her own bedroom in the front of the house. When she died in February of 1960, the house served as the Raymer's residence.

Center room,
Red Barn Studio, 1998.
Photo by Jim Richardson.

Raymer's collection of
Mexican earthenware,
Red Barn Studio collection.

By this time, the Red Barn Craft Studio had become the Red Barn Studio. When the white house became their home, Raymer utilized the original studio for storing auction treasures and as a work space for large commission pieces. The north side, which had been their home, became Raymer's main studio work space. By 1961 Raymer began major remodeling of the kitchen space in the studio. He added another heater in the back work room so that, "...I can work over there without having to heat the whole studio." He moved his work room back to the barn area for the summers.

The center section of the Red Barn Studio evolved in the late 1960s. In the fall of 1968 Raymer wrote to Greer, "A pan figure was carved and placed on the beam above this fireplace." In January of 1969, Raymer also wrote about it to Smith, stating, "Did a wood carving of Pan and his pipes, a bracket to support the large beam that runs above the alcove for the fireplace." In September of 1968 Raymer wrote to Smith, "My painting is at a standstill, the bathroom has taken precedence." A new roof was put on the studio garage in 1969. The rest of the studio was roofed that summer.

As the studio grew and changed, Raymer pondered what to put in each space. His mind kept searching for things he needed and wanted to complete the studio. Raymer continued to collect items from his friends, auctions, garage sales, special "finds," and by visiting demolition sites. Special items came to Raymer through trades with Margaret Greenough. Her husband, Pelham Greenough, collected special furniture and crafts in his travels abroad. Margaret traded some of these items with Raymer for his artwork. Then the two would talk about how the other got the best deal and how, maybe, they should trade back.

26

In later life, both Raymer and his wife began experiencing health problems. Depression, brought on by this and Lester's first heart attack, changed the focus of the Red Barn Studio. After 1975, Raymer's promotion of his work fluctuated; sometimes he focused on art production and sometimes on remodeling the studio. There were periods of time throughout the remainder of his life that Raymer's health kept him from working on his art at all. Festival crowds seemed too much for him. Ramona Raymer was not always able to greet the guests, so for several years the studio was closed. Yet in 1979, Raymer wrote to Smith that he planned to be open for HyllningsFest and that he had "17 new oils and a dozen or so drawings." In the 1980s the focus of Raymer's art work turned, for the most part, away from participating in community festivals to production for exhibitions and sales at the Könstverk Gallery. When Dale Hoag started the Könstverk Art Gallery in 1980, Raymer turned the majority of his work over to Hoag.

By the mid 1970s, Raymer was determined to move to the original Red Barn Studio space and find some way to maintain the other space. He began, in 1975, to remodel the south side of the studio and dispose of some things. He tells Smith, "Incredible how people came and carried things away, almost everything (referring to a sale he and Ramona had). Lan (Nelson) got here mid-May and he and I started almost immediately to remodel the little barn into another studio apartment. I have a huge north window, part of the loft was taken out much like in the main studio. Put a new roof on, got quite a lot done, sheet rocked the ceiling, installed old weathered barn wood paneling, a new inside stairway, etc, etc."

The windows Raymer talks about for the south studio were obtained from friends, sales, or "found." When he was ready to install a window, Raymer just cut the opening and inserted the window, keeping it in place by nailing it to the casements. Raymer wrote to Smith in 1977 that the addition to the studio (south side of current studio) had progressed, "a brick floor was added, a Franklin stove placed in the east wall and a gas wall heater on the west wall." Eventually, part of the walls were covered with sections of an old garage door Raymer got from a friend and other old doors he obtained from the Brunswick.

By 1977 it was the remodeling of the studio that frustrated Raymer. "My painting has been sadly neglected, but the building project is more or

Winter view, Red Barn Studio.

Early interior studio photographs.

27

less complete." The burden of the studio and sales often frustrated Raymer. Yet he continued to generate a good income from his work. He remarks, "Why does life have to be so damn complicated?"

Obviously, from letters written in October of 1978, the remodeling was still in progress, "...but it is going slowly." Raymer indicates to Smith that he plans to use the redone space as a studio and keep the lean-to garage as a storage area. He states, "I would use only that space and rent or sell the other part of the Red Barn Studio." Raymer tells Smith that he is growing weary and that both he and Ramona have been ill frequently. He laments, "It is harder and harder to cope with everything. The studio will soon be a burden. There are three options," Raymer indicated, "sell it, rent it, or just close it down." The options also included "...that Dr. Struxness, a friend, might move in. I had considered Lan Nelson having it but Lan has purchased a home." Raymer concludes by asking Larry Smith if he would be interested in having the studio.

> *"Life is just one crisis after another. I wonder what to do with all the stuff. I will hate to part with some of it. At some point in time, posses-sions seem to become if not a burden, certainly a problem. Possibly the only solution is to get rid of them."*

Over a period of years in the 1980s, Raymer disposed of, in his terms, "junk" from the studio on a regular basis. At one point in 1981 he wrote, "Maybe I should have an auction." He was still concerned about everything in December of 1982, "More and more it's getting to be a chore holding body and soul together." He talks about ideas related to everything they own, "We live with these things. Every nook, cranny, and cabinet is filled with these things, they are a part of our life." In 1983 Raymer was still pondering his possessions, "Hauling away termite wood and junk but still a lot of stuff."

"Now Smith, the studio needs a lot of work. Maybe the floor could have Mexican tile, maybe storm windows, maybe replace the furnace," Raymer wrote in September of 1981. He indicates that ideas for the renovation of the studio were discussed with Dale Hoag. Letters Raymer wrote to Smith in the 1980s were filled with ideas and assurances to entice Smith to move to the Red Barn Studio.

In 1986, Rick Nelson, a building contractor from Salina, Kansas, purchased the Könstverk Gallery from Hoag and continued to represent Raymer. The gallery had a number of Raymer shows and sales continued. Nelson encouraged Raymer to keep creating artwork, bringing art supplies

Ramona and Lester Raymer in the Birger Sandzén Memorial Gallery at the Raymer Retrospective, 1988.

to him on a regular basis. He also began to assist Raymer with changing the studio to a place for visitors to come on special occasions. Things were reorganized. Some of the toys were even brought from the house to the studio, so that the studio was once again a place for the public to visit. Nelson became a friend of Raymer, constantly encouraging him in his artwork.

The concerns related to the future of the Red Barn Studio and Raymer's artwork led to a variety of proposed solutions. In addition to someone taking care of the studio, there was the issue of the artwork. Several national museums made offers for the toy collection and some of the artwork. Bankers in Lindsborg and Salina, Kansas, worked with Raymer on ideas designed to keep the toy collection in the region. Dale Hoag, Rick Nelson, Don Weddle, and other friends participated in lengthy discussions with the Raymers. The final result was the founding of the Raymer Society. Local lawyers assisted the Raymers and their friends in designing the nonprofit organization which received its 501 3-C status in 1986. The mission of the Raymer Society, determined by the Raymers in conversations with their friends, was to preserve the Red Barn Studio as a museum and to provide cultural programming. This decision brought to rest a troublesome burden for Raymer. It gave direction to his life again, freeing him to focus on his creative visions.

In 1990, Ramona moved to Bethany Home, an intermediate care facility in Lindsborg. Raymer originally planned to move with Ramona. He helped her settle in, visited her regularly, but never made the move himself. With the help of many special friends who brought him meals and took care of his needs, Raymer was able to maintain a limited schedule of working in the studio up to his death.

Lester Raymer died June 1, 1991.
Ramona Raymer died July 12 , 1992.

29

Lester's work table in
Red Barn Studio
with unfinished painting.
Photo by Jim Richardson,1998.

In 1988 the Raymer Society began functioning as a volunteer organization responsible for studio open houses during special events. When Lester Raymer died, the society became the full-time caretakers of the Red Barn Studio and the Raymer residence. When Ramona Raymer died, the total estate of the Raymers became property of the Raymer Society. The Raymer and Weddle families received personal family items as a part of the estate settlement.

Limited restoration of the Red Barn Studio was completed from 1991-1993. In 1993, the board of directors made the decision to begin major restoration of the Red Barn Studio. In the spring of 1994, the board of directors hired Dr. Carla Scott as the first executive director. The executive director's position was upgraded to a full-time position in January, 1997. Scott's first day of work coincided with the moving of all the art and artifacts from the Red Barn Studio into the Raymers' home so that restoration could begin. During the course of the restoration, many walls came down and were replaced. Extensive termite damage necessitated new floor and wall construction. Patios were re-bricked and the dilapidated front brick fence was reconstructed. In 1998 the front garage space was converted to an art research library, preserving the historical exterior.

When visitors enter the Red Barn Studio today they are immediately taken by the wealth of things to view. Walking through the studio, visitors remark that this artist must never have been idle. They wonder at the ability of one person to create such a volume and diversity of art with so unique a quality. They are overwhelmed by the artistic achievement when they realize that the studio houses only a small fraction of the work Raymer completed. One customer wrote back to the Raymers in 1966 saying, "Your house is a little jewel and reminds me of tours of houses in Europe. We cherish the little rooster we purchased. It looks so proud and strong." Peggy of the Flint Hills, a writer for the *Topeka Capital-Journal,* said in her May 1967 article that "the studio has the richness of a museum." Just over thirty years later, on September 27, 1997, the Red Barn Studio restoration was complete and her projection became a reality.

Lester Raymer and his Art World

Bruce R. Kahler

Among the many newspaper clippings concerning her husband's career that Ramona Raymer preserved is a short article from the *Topeka* (Kansas) *Daily Capital* dated March 1, 1956. It is a regular column whose author, Zula Bennington (Peggy) Greene, is identified with the byline "Peggy of the Flint Hills."[1]

Greene has some news to convey. Lester Raymer's woodcarving of St. Francis, purchased the year before by Topeka's Mulvane Art Center, has been loaned to the Des Moines (Iowa) Art Center for an exhibition to be held in conjunction with the national convention of the American Federation of Art. She is clearly intrigued by her fellow Kansan who has received this honor. She thinks Raymer is not just a skilled worker but also "quiet, genuine, and not a little inscrutable." Furthermore, he is appreciated by other local artists. The head of the Washburn University Art Department, Alexander Tillotson, had mentioned to Greene that he was "impressed by (Raymer's) quick perception and the excellence of his judgment." Bernard Stone, a young Topeka artist who was studying in Taos, New Mexico, recently expressed to her his admiration of Raymer's work.[2]

At first glance this little report might appear to be solely a description of Lester Raymer's growing reputation. Greene tells us that his work has received the stamp of approval of both institutions and individuals, established and emerging artists, people familiar with art in Topeka and in Taos. She summarizes: "Raymer is an artist whose concentration of sincerity and fundamental soundness is reaching farther and farther from his home studio of the Red Barn in Lindsborg."[3]

But surely, Greene recognized that to the potential buyers of art among her readers, word of an artist's growing reputation serves a prescriptive function too. She is, in effect, telling such people that now is the time to take notice of this skillful and enigmatic Lester Raymer, to visit his studio, and to purchase his work. "Peggy of the Flint Hills" has written not only a brief news item and opinion piece, but also a promotional message.

Just over a year earlier Greene had written a long feature article on Raymer. She would write several more about him over the next two decades. She would, in fact, become his most important champion in the press. Along with this came friendship. Greene passed along privately to the Raymers the favorable comments that eventually appeared in her March 1956 column. In her 1955 Christmas card she quoted Bernard Stone directly as saying that Lester "was about the best artist in this part of the country."[4] She also explained in another letter why she had described Raymer as "inscrutable." "Mr. Tillotson, when I expressed admiration for you, said, 'I don't know him very well—he's not easy to know.'"[5]

Untitled, clown torso with circus tent, oil on masonite, 1962, Raymer Society Collection, gift from Peter and Irene Kennedy.

As friend and sympathetic journalist, Peggy Greene made a significant contribution to the development of Raymer's career. She was one of many individuals and organizations that Raymer came to depend upon for support. In this sense, Greene was a part of Raymer's "art world," the network of people whose cooperation was necessary for the making of and then the using of, his art.[6]

It is common today to conceive of the artist, in the true sense, as a creative genius who sees more clearly and feels more deeply than normal human beings. An artist, the argument goes, is thoroughly preoccupied with the issues and traditions of art and therefore lives in a world apart from ordinary circumstances. A heroic individualist, the artist is a radically free and independent person who transcends the concerns of the times. A few of Raymer's admirers have claimed that he was a "genius." He was, they believed, a remarkably prolific and multifaceted man who displayed a universality of mind and a powerful urge to create art for its own sake, not for

34

money or fame.[7] Raymer contributed to this interpretation of his own behavior. He believed his work was superior to that of all other artists in the Lindsborg area. Throughout the years he never quite embraced the town he had adopted, remaining ambivalent about its value as a creative environment. Raymer was also very selective in his choice of friends and his natural reticence, exaggerated in later years by increasing deafness, tended to isolate him. All of this lent a detached aura to the man.

This account of Lester Raymer's career, however, is not a story about some solitary genius. He was an exceptional artist and an unusually creative soul. But Raymer was also a man with connections; he was an artist related to others either by necessity or through choice. One can understand him best, therefore, not by isolating him from and elevating him above his circumstances, but by situating him within his social context. Raymer was at the center of an art world that reached outward from his wife and the studio they had built together to the town of Lindsborg, Kansas, with its college and other artists, studios and galleries. Going beyond this base of interrelationships, Raymer gained further attention and support from newspapers, magazines, customers and patrons throughout the Midwest and the nation.

In the end, there is Raymer's reputation as an artist, what the inhabitants of his art world thought of him, how they defined his importance. Although he was always a very versatile artist, working in several media, Raymer's reputation, after moving to Lindsborg, evolved through four fairly distinct phases. During the late 1940s and early 1950s, he was known primarily as a ceramist. He chose to make pottery and ceramic sculptures because selling such work enabled him to make a living. Raymer thought of himself, first and foremost, as a painter and, indeed, this was how the public saw him by the mid-1950s. Religious subjects began to dominate his work and he received several commissions from churches to make metal and mosaic sculptures. These, along with smaller items he sent to exhibitions in the early 1960s, generated a national reputation for Raymer. After abruptly discontinuing this very demanding work, he settled down again to his painting and a variety of other pursuits. During the 1970s and 1980s he was known chiefly to the wider public for the growing collection of Christmas toys that he made each year for Ramona.

IT'S ALL I'VE EVER DONE AND WANTED TO DO

Lester Wilton Raymer was born on September 24, 1907, on a farm outside Alva, Oklahoma.[8] He was the second of three sons belonging to John C. and Carolyn Erb Raymer.[9] Although he had little interest in recounting the details of his childhood, Raymer did insist on one point—he had always wanted to be an artist. "An artist is born, not made," he once told a newspaper reporter: "It's all I've ever done and wanted to do. Even as a child, I was drawing, painting, dabbling at it. Probably as a child, I made a decision to be an artist." He claimed that when he was only a few years old he had copied a picture of the Madonna. At age ten he entered a drawing in a children's art competition at the county fair, only to have it disqualified by judges who thought it was so good that an adult must have made it.[10]

About the time Raymer was thirteen or fourteen the family moved north to Aurora, Colorado, in search of a climate more congenial to his father's tuberculosis.[11] "Red," as Raymer was known at the time, was one of Aurora High School's most outstanding students. He was elected vice-president of his junior class, impressed basketball fans as "probably the best guard ever developed at Aurora High,"[12] and in his senior year when students voted, "either seriously or as a joke," for the most popular boy, Raymer received the dubious honor. The 1927 school yearbook also commended him as "an artist of more than ordinary ability" whose work had appeared in a number of student publications.[13]

Sometime during high school Raymer decided he wanted to pursue his interests at the School of the Art Institute of Chicago. He had saved enough money by the fall of 1930 to pay his first year's tuition.[14] In recognition of his abilities as a painter, particularly in composition, the school awarded him the Anna Louise Raymond Scholarship for the next three years.[15] The Raymond Scholarship, grading papers for noted art historian Helen Gardner, author of

Section Page design for 1927 High School yearbook, Raymer Society Collection.

Thanks to Birgit Hegewald for 1997 research to locate this.

36

the textbook *Art Through the Ages*, and working as a janitor enabled Raymer
to support himself in the big city.[16]

Raymer had arrived in Chicago seventeen years after the controversial,
yet highly influential, Armory Show introduced the city to the modernist art
of Europe. Nevertheless, the School of the Art Institute still remained a
bastion of conservative art training. Charlotte Moser argues that "reverence
for the antique and the idealized depiction of the human figure, for the technical expertise of past masters, for the image of the Renaissance artist as a
worldly *homme d' affaires* had permeated School curriculum since its founding in 1866."[17] During the 1920s a few visiting artists from New York's
Ashcan School, including George Bellows, introduced students and faculty to
their distinctive brand of social realism and personal expression. Even then
the School of the Art Institute's genteel academism changed only slowly and
painfully into a more contemporary attitude toward art.[18]

Fleeting and insubstantial as it may have been, this spirit of reform was
still able to reach Raymer. He was among those students who met regularly
at the home of Kathleen Blackshear, protégé of Helen Gardner.[19] The teaching of art history and inquiry into the philosophical implications of past art
had been inaugurated under Gardner only in 1920. Before that the School's
administrators had believed these subjects were too difficult for students.[20]
Raymer was introduced to a Russian brand of modernism when he painted
for a year and a half under the direction of Boris Anisfeld.[21] Anisfeld had
joined the faculty of the school in 1929 and was known for his expressionis-
tic use of color, especially in theatrical set designs.[22]

Raymer was not destined to finish his degree at the School of the Art
Institute of Chicago. His father died suddenly while visiting him in Chicago in
October 1933. Raymer withdrew from his studies and returned to the family

Top half of page:
Woodcut illustrations for
"Muleshoe Ballads of
Oklahoma Bob,"
ca 1935.

Bottom half of page:
Woodcut illustrations from
Munson Hatchery promotion,
designed by Lester Raymer,
Oklahoma, ca 1947,
Raymer Society Archives.

HUSKY POULTS
from Oklahoma Free-Range Flocks
U. S. Approved—Pullorum Controlled
* * *
Munson
MISTLETOE
Bronze and Small Whites
* * *
Munson Hatchery
Established 1928
Phone 1402   ALVA, OKLA.

farm near Alva.[23] This turn of events was, of course, a serious blow to his ambitions, and yet during the next twelve years he would succeed in building a reputation as an artist in northern Oklahoma.

He began by setting up a studio and living quarters at the Raymer farm. He slept much of the day but also helped with the lighter farm chores and raised turkeys for money. On the first floor studio he pursued his artwork during the night. In Oklahoma Raymer continued to draw and to paint; however, his creative energy seemed to explode in all directions as he expressed himself in a variety of other media as well. Family members recall that he carved wood, painted furniture, sandcast concrete sculptures, quilted, crocheted, made linoleum block prints, and used a small blacksmith forge that had belonged to his father.[24]

Determined to continue his education, Raymer attended classes at Northwestern State College in Alva. Coursework in history, Spanish, and several other fields supplemented his previous art credits, thus enabling him to receive a bachelor of fine arts degree from the School of the Art Institute of Chicago.[25] Also during these years Raymer found an enthusiastic local patron in Marjorie Sawyer-Munson. Munson purchased his paintings and made her home available for an exhibition of his work.[26] She asked Raymer to illustrate her book, *Muleshoe Ballads of Oklahoma Bob,*[27] and, in later years, the promotional pamphlet and stationery for the family-operated turkey hatchery.[28]

Then there was the important task of developing a reputation in the larger world. For Raymer, at this early stage of his career, that meant Oklahoma. He presented himself as a painter and focused his efforts on gaining recognition in Tulsa, the largest city in the northern part of the state. Raymer's first big splash of recognition came late in 1937 when his painting *In the Ring* was exhibited in the Eighth Annual Oklahoma Artists Exhibit

Top: Untitled, Ramona, oil on canvas, ca 1946, private collection.

Bottom: Incidental illustration from "Muleshoe Ballads."

39

sponsored by the Tulsa Art Association. His work won the Mrs. Eugene Lorton Gold Medal as best entry in the show and also a separate purchase prize.[29] Throughout the early 1940s, Raymer regularly participated in annual exhibitions at the Philbrook Art Center, also in Tulsa. In 1944, for example, *Three Joeys,* a piece he would show often throughout the decade, received the second prize in oils.[30]

HAND IN HAND WITH DAILY LIVING

Raymer did make one attempt to show his art outside the bounds of his home state. At the town of Lindsborg, located about 120 miles due north of Alva, Bethany College had been holding its Midwest Art Exhibition every Holy Week since 1899.[31] In 1942 Raymer contributed work to the exhibition which was displayed in the Swedish Pavilion, the site for art instruction on the College's campus.[32] That same year, he was also honored with a one-man show in the north wing of the building.[33]

After he had sent work to the next two "Easter Shows" the local newspaper, the *Lindsborg News-Record,* began to notice that Raymer was spending considerable time in town.[34] The paper's review of the 1945 Midwest Art Exhibition officially introduced Raymer to the community. It presented him as an award-winning graduate of Chicago's Art Institute who, though not a resident of Lindsborg, was well known in the area. The *News-Record* commented on the wide variety of Raymer's contributions to that year's show, not only portraits and other paintings, but also wood carvings, jewelry, and even an old gun and powder horn he had decorated.[35]

The piece of art by Raymer that particularly caught the eye of the exhibition's reviewer was a full-sized portrait of Lindsborg native Ramona Weddle and her dog. Here, most certainly, was evidence of why Raymer had

become so familiar to this small town in central Kansas. He had met
Ramona in the fall of 1930 when they were both new students at the School
of the Art Institute of Chicago.[36] She was the daughter of one of Lindsborg's
most prominent citizens, Edgar M. Weddle, proprietor of the Brunswick
Hotel.[37] Before she had gone to Chicago, Ramona had attended classes at
Bethany College and then later at Kansas State College in Manhattan,
Kansas.[38] We do not know the full nature of the relationship between Lester
and Ramona during the decade between his leaving Chicago in 1933 and
his first appearance on the Lindsborg art scene. We can assume, however,
that over the next few years their bond grew strong for it culminated in
marriage on October 12, 1945.[39]

Raymer set up his studio in the Brunswick Hotel. These were temporary
quarters, however, for he and Ramona soon began constructing their own living
and working spaces on the lot directly south of the hotel. They accomplished
this by using two structures that belonged to the Brunswick: a laundry building
and a carriage barn. The laundry became the Raymers' home, the barn Lester's
studio. The studio also included a workroom for Ramona's father.[40]

Early visitors to the Raymers found the "Red Barn," as the home/studio
was called, as worthy of comment as Lester and his art. In fact, the man and
his setting became virtually indistinguishable. Raymer had created a physical environment that perfectly illustrated his versatility. "The amazing thing
about the new home," said the *News-Record*, "is that Lester Raymer has
done nearly all the work himself with the aid and advice of his talented
wife."[41] An article in *to the Stars* magazine suggested that the Red Barn was

"striking testimony that the young artist wields a hammer and saw as well as he handles a palette."[42] Raymer himself seemed pleased with this demonstration of his ingenuity. He was especially proud of the fact that he had used no new materials in the building's construction. "It is an experiment in making something out of nothing, " he suggested, with a bit of hyperbole.[43]

Everyone recognized that the Red Barn had a special quality about it. Raymer had put his stamp on the place, covering its walls and filling its corners with his work. One felt the uniqueness of the place. Bob Nelson, a columnist for the *Salina Journal*, declared Raymer's studio "a 'must' for those who like their atmosphere in huge servings."[44] For one visitor that atmosphere was "colonial,"[45] for another it was "Swedish peasant."[46]

As word about the Raymers' new home/studio spread, it quickly became a popular destination of innumerable individuals and groups. A visit to the Red Barn became an absolute necessity for anyone in central Kansas interested in the arts. Among the most frequent pilgrims were the many civic organizations that could be found in even the smallest Kansas towns. The Raymers' records indicate that in one ten-month period, for example, they were host to the Moundridge Study Club, the Women's Home Culture Club of Hope, Kansas, the Marquette Women's Literary Club, the Valley Center Progressive Women's Club, and the Kansas Home Demonstration Agent's Association.[47]

Ramona was in charge of guiding visitors through the Red Barn. It was a role she assumed cheerfully, but also with great seriousness. When the president of Marquette's literary club asked if Ramona could visit them and talk about art, she replied:

> *"We feel that to talk intelligently on Art to the layman requires a certain gift, a great deal of preparation, and the necessity of being able to show examples. The examples perhaps being the most important of all. Therefore I am declining your invitation to visit and talk to your club, and am offering a counter proposal—an invitation to your group to come to Lindsborg and visit our home and studio...where we will endeavor to explain and show the various arts and crafts with which we work."[48]*

Of course, Lester was a part of the show. No doubt most guests hoped to see not only the art he had made, but also the artist himself, at work. He remained ambivalent, however, about this aspect of life at the Red Barn. In a letter to his best friend, Milford Greer, Raymer mentioned that in recent days he had received at least a dozen letters from groups who wanted to drop by the studio. "Where will this lead to?" he asked rhetorically.[49] It became for him a matter of separating, as he said, the "wheat" from the "chaff."[50] He rejoiced when visited by intelligent and expressive people, such as the students from Kansas State College who called one spring day ("a more enthusiastic and interested group of vital young people one couldn't find anywhere")[51] or J. Sheldon Carey, a professor of ceramics at the University of Kansas, with whom he talked for hours. With obvious excitement Raymer wrote to Greer about the conversation with Carey: "How nice it would be to have visitors like that oftener.[sic] A meeting of ideas, stimulating contacts. I treasure every one and hoard them carefully to tide me over the lean days."[52] And yet, all too often, Raymer was exasperated by an "endless stream of callers."[53] He simply did not feel very productive when "swarms of people" constantly interrupted his work.[54]

Detail with Red Barn Studio - from Lester's map of Lindsborg created for the Artists' Guild.

"I am a foreigner from Oklahoma," Raymer facetiously told an interviewer, shortly after moving to the area. But the reporter, coming from the nearby town of McPherson, knew that Raymer would easily fit into local society. "He is typical of Lindsborg, where the ability to create something beautiful goes hand in hand with daily living."[55] Raymer was settling down into a small and geographically isolated community, but one renowned for its devotion to culture.

The focus of art activity in the town (outside the Bethany College campus) during Raymer's first decade there was the Lindsborg Artists' Guild. Dolores Gaston Runbeck founded the organization when she called together a group of artist friends and acquaintances to her house early in October 1949.[56] Runbeck, known for her watercolor paintings of flowers, had studied art at Bethany and at the Chicago School of Applied Arts. She was also the National Alumni President of Delta Phi Delta, the national honorary art fraternity. Among the other fourteen charter members of the guild were her sister Lucille, a ceramist who had taught at Washburn University and in local public schools; Anton Pearson, who made humorous woodcarvings of everyday people from Sweden; Alba Malm, school teacher and painter of landscapes; Oscar Gunnarson, proprietor of the local paint store who painted snow scenes and Swedish figurines; Signe Larson, a Bethany graduate whose portrait head of Christ *Thy Kingdom Come* had become a national favorite; and both Lester and Ramona Raymer.[57]

Privately, Lester had serious misgivings about the guild. He saw little value in the group's meetings, telling Milford Greer that he could not "imagine

Map of Lindsborg, drawn by Lester Raymer, showing the locations of homes and studios of members of the Lindsborg Artists' Guild for Guild brochure, ca 1949, Raymer Society Archives.

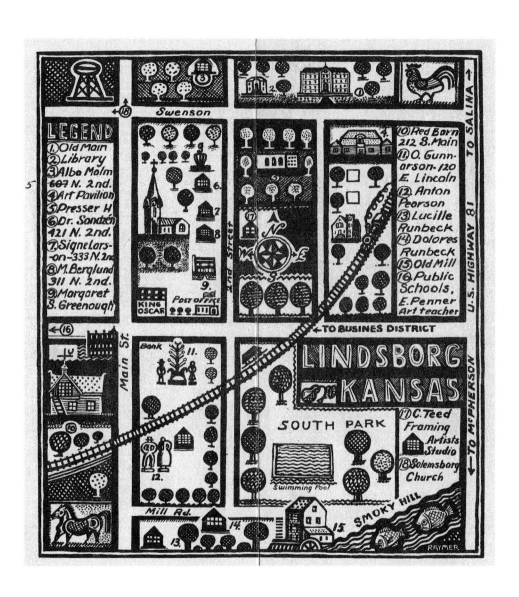

a more fruitless way to spend an evening."[58] The collection of artists that Runbeck had gathered struck him as "pitiful" and left him skeptical about the possibility of intellectual stimulation in Lindsborg:

> *"The futility of it all is almost frightening to me Milford. The life here seemingly so little-empty-futile. Can one become desperate enough to do something about it? It is possible I think–when one begins to doubt and question the validity of ones [sic] work then it is no good. The incentive is choked off, ideas die unborn."[59]*

Nevertheless, Raymer participated in the guild's efforts to promote Lindsborg as a tourist site for art lovers. A pamphlet produced by the group included a quaint little map of the town, drawn by Raymer, to locate the studios and houses of guild members.[60]

The pamphlet also noted that there was a considerable amount of artwork in Lindsborg in dire need of permanent housing. For example, Oscar Thorsen, long-time piano instructor at Bethany, owned a large collection of paintings, antique furniture, bronzes by Swedish sculptor Carl Milles, and Oriental art that he was willing to bequeath to Lindsborg provided the town adequately preserved it.[61] The Artists' Guild argued that the construction of a gallery for this and other collections "would be highly justified if not an absolute necessity."[62]

Seven years later Lindsborg met this need. A new edition of the organization's flyer had on its cover a photograph of the new Birger Sandzén Memorial Gallery.[63] The recently deceased Birger Sandzén (1871-1954) was an artist of national fame and the presiding figure in Lindsborg's art world. The town and Bethany College, where he taught for 52 years, possessed the reputation they had in the arts primarily because of Sandzén's enormous energy and skill as a painter, writer, speaker, and organizer of artists.[64] In 1955 a memorial foundation was established in Sandzén's name, and then two years later, the gallery was opened to the public. Both accomplishments were largely the result of the efforts and financial support of Sandzén's son-in-law, Charles Pelham Greenough 3d.[65]

The Sandzén Gallery immediately became a chief center of art activity in Lindsborg. Although its primary mission was to place Birger Sandzén's art on permanent display, the gallery also sponsored touring exhibitions and regularly showed work by local and regional artists. A selection of sixteen oil paintings by Raymer, thematically focused on the circus and on the life of

Christ, was the first exhibition at the new facility to feature an artist other than Sandzén.[66] Raymer frequently lent his pieces to the gallery as soon as he finished them, and before they traveled to their final destination.[67] On occasion, he even donated items to the gallery's permanent collection.[68] After 1969, during the final phase of Raymer's career, hardly a year passed when the Gallery did not feature his work or at least include it in its exhibitions.[69] In 1988 it organized a major retrospective of the artist's career.[69] No other institution played a more important role in keeping Raymer's art on view during the last quarter-century of his life.

Shortly after the Sandzén Gallery opened, a regular column, "Art Gallery Notes," began to appear in the *Lindsborg News-Record*. The author was Margaret Sandzén Greenough, daughter of the artist and wife of Charles Pelham Greenough. Greenough had studied art with her father at Bethany, spent a year in a Parisian art school *Les Trois Ateliers*, and then after a teaching stint back home at the College, continued her studies in New York at the Art Students' League and Columbia University.[70] She was now thoroughly committed to preserving the memory of her father, but not at the expense of other artists' reputations. Greenough recognized and applauded the fact that Raymer's art appealed to an audience that her father's "missionary work" had not reached.[71] She became one of Raymer's most enthusiastic supporters.

For Greenough, Raymer was "a person of extraordinary talent and ability,"[72] and she told her readers she believed anything he chose to paint had merit.[73] Intent as she was to show Raymer's art at the Sandzén Gallery, Greenough was perhaps even more eager to purchase his work for her

46

personal collection. A steady stream of brief notes to Raymer indicates that she constantly struggled to keep up payments on items she just had to buy from him on credit.[74] When Raymer gave her a gift of his own work, Greenough was ecstatic. "I just cannot thank you enough for that beautiful painting! It has so much life and interesting painting in it - it's so spontaneous but organized! I love it! Thank you from the bottom of my heart."[75]

The new Sandzén Gallery attracted the attention of journalists from larger cities in the region. Upon visiting Lindsborg they were impressed by the exceptional amount of arts activity in the town and the distinctive tenor of life that resulted. A reporter from Wichita observed that, because culture so permeated the atmosphere of Lindsborg, no matter where he turned he found "someone with more interest in art than in making money."[76] Similarly, a visitor from the *Kansas City Star* thought it remarkable that the Sandzén Gallery was larger than any business building in town. Noting how cultural events in Lindsborg "transcended any small-town attitudes," he suggested that open-mindedness accompanied a devotion to the arts.[77]

The Birger Sandzén Memorial Gallery, Lindsborg, Kansas, open to the public in 1957. Photo from Birger Sandzén Memorial Gallery Archives.

Lindsborg's reputation for being devoted to the arts continued to develop throughout the next three decades. One measure of this devotion was the sheer number of artists in town. In 1967 a writer from Topeka lamented that her home town of approximately 100,000 residents, had fewer artists who made their living solely through the sale of their work than Lindsborg with a population of under twenty-four hundred.[78] Fifteen years later the *Salina Journal* reported that one percent of adult workers in Lindsborg were professional artists, five times the national percentage.[79]

While everyone seemed to agree that Lindsborg was home to an unusually large number of artists and the site of many cultural events, there was no similar consensus concerning the relationship between the arts and the town's life in general. Some people thought of Lindsborg as an "art colony."[80] It was a special community that was "artistic down to the very core,"[81] unique in all of Kansas. Joanna K. Wiebe proposed in the *Wichita Eagle and Beacon* that Lindsborg was attractive to an artist or craftsperson in part because there were so many other expressive souls to interact with and also because of the town's "ivory tower isolation from influences disruptive to the creative process."[82]

Others, however, were eager to avoid the "ivory tower" image and instead emphasize, as the reporter from McPherson had, that the arts went

*The Silent Stream,
by Birger Sandzén,
linoleum cut on paper, 1931.
Used for cover of Lindsborg
Artists' Guild brochure, 1949,
from Birger Sandzén Memorial
Gallery Archives.*

"hand in hand with daily living." "Lindsborg artists are not exotics" insisted a brochure promoting "Open House 70s," a nonprofit association of local artists which encouraged the public to visit its members in their work sites and showplaces. The text elaborated: "Passionate about the ever-renewed attempt to shape crude material into art, we are also cordial men and women who enjoy agreeable conversation as you stop on your rounds of our studios and galleries."[83] Kay Berenson agreed. Writing for the Salina newspaper, she argued that Lindsborg artists were not "bohemians" but hardworking middle-class citizens. They, like so many artists elsewhere, had to make compromises "either to hold down regular jobs in addition to their art work or to do 'commercial' as well as 'real' art."[84]

VERY MUCH UPSET AND MORE THAN A LITTLE PUZZLED

At the end of the spring 1946 term, Bethany College announced that its most distinguished faculty member, Birger Sandzén, had resigned as head of the Art Department but would continue to serve as artist-in-residence.[85] For over half a century Sandzén had been a consummate professional artist. More than a prolific and distinctive landscape painter and printmaker, he was also deeply imbued with a service ethic that took him outside the studio. Sandzén was devoted to purely aesthetic concerns, but he also possessed a strong sense of civic responsibility. For this reason, he was not just an artist but a professor of art, and he taught not only the usual art courses but Romance languages, voice lessons, and art history as well. He wrote articles for newspapers and magazines, exhibited his art and spoke to public gatherings, and helped establish organizations such as the Kansas Federation of Art, the Prairie Print Makers, the Smoky Hill Art Club, and Bethany's chapter of Delta Phi Delta. Birger Sandzén's greatest contribution, therefore, was to the cause of art appreciation.[86]

Sandzén's retirement obviously left a huge gap in Bethany's teaching staff. One might have expected the college to search for a new professor of substantial achievement to fill it. Instead, perhaps because of the late date of Sandzén's announcement, the Bethany administration offered a one-year contract to Lindsborg newcomer Lester Raymer. As instructor in art he had the responsibility of teaching drawing and painting.[87]

Over the course of the 1946-47 school year, occasional references to Raymer in the *Bethany Messenger*, the college's newspaper, suggest that he

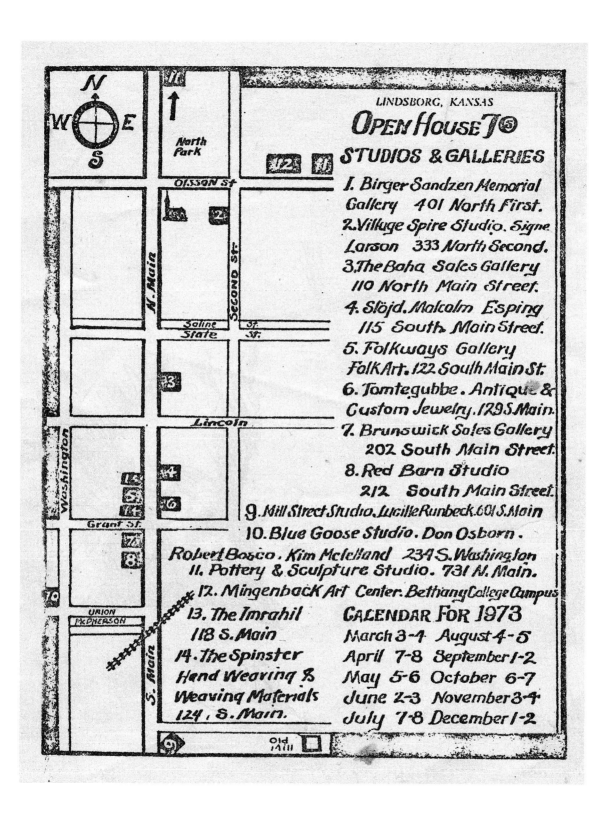

LINDSBORG, KANSAS

OPEN HOUSE 70

STUDIOS & GALLERIES

1. Birger Sandzen Memorial Gallery 401 North First.
2. Village Spire Studio, Signe Larson 333 North Second.
3. The Boha Sales Gallery 110 North Main Street.
4. Slöjd, Malcolm Esping 115 South Main Street.
5. Folkways Gallery Folk Art. 122 South Main St.
6. Tomtegubbe. Antique & Custom Jewelry. 129 S. Main.
7. Brunswick Sales Gallery 202 South Main Street.
8. Red Barn Studio 212 South Main Street.
9. Mill Street Studio. Lucille Runbeck. 601 S. Main
10. Blue Goose Studio. Don Osborn. Robert Bosco. Kim McClelland 234 S. Washington
11. Pottery & Sculpture Studio. 731 N. Main.
12. Mingenback Art Center. Bethany College Campus
13. The Imrahil 118 S. Main
14. The Spinster Hand Weaving & Weaving Materials 124 S. Main.

CALENDAR FOR 1973

March 3-4   August 4-5
April 7-8   September 1-2
May 5-6   October 6-7
June 2-3   November 3-4
July 7-8   December 1-2

Open House flyer, designed and drawn by Lester Raymer, 1973, Raymer Society Archives.

fit in well with campus life. He was welcomed into Delta Phi Delta as an honorary member,[88] contributed work to the Smoky Hill Art Club's annual print sale, [89] and showed several paintings and woodcarvings at the Midwest Art Exhibition.[90] Raymer also joined other professors on a short trip to Salina to see the Kansas City Philharmonic Orchestra in concert,[91] and participated in a meeting of the Faculty Club held at Oscar Thorsen's apartment.[92] Nothing out of the ordinary here, and yet, beneath the placid surface there was serious trouble.

On April 17, 1947, Raymer received the shocking news that he could not return the next year to teach at Bethany. The college's president, Emory Lindquist, informed Raymer that, while his "work professionally and personally has been the finest in every respect," the Art Department would replace him with Charles Rogers. At issue for Lindquist was Raymer's lack of a master's degree. "I have felt," he wrote to Raymer, "that whenever possible we should staff our positions with graduate degrees. I recognize that a graduate degree is not always the decisive factor in effective teaching, but it is a factor in our educational arrangements."[93] Lindquist may have betrayed a certain defensiveness about his stance on sufficient credentials, but he remained firm in his decision.

"Needless to say I am very much upset and more than a little puzzled at the course of events,"[94] Raymer replied in a letter to Lindquist two days later. Yet, it would appear that the question of the master's degree had been raised earlier. Raymer had inquired about the requirements for the master of fine arts degree at the School of the Art Institute of Chicago more than a month before Lindquist's announcement.[95] And, in his response to Bethany's president, Raymer pointed out that he had recently applied to the graduate program at the University of New Mexico. Since he liked teaching and had done it well, he found it difficult to fathom why other factors could not be considered, such as his commitment to living in Lindsborg and his reputation as an artist who gave "some promise of going on to bigger and better things." Raymer also reminded Lindquist that Ramona had come to the president's assistance several times, perhaps referring to her temporary teaching assignments in the Art Department in 1943 and 1945. To show his continuing interest in the art program at Bethany, Raymer suggested that problems of "inadequate curriculum" and lack of facilities and equipment could be overcome. He proposed new courses in composition and anatomy.[96]

Raymer seems to have believed that there was one other possible reason, besides his not having a master's degree, for Lindquist's surprising decision. Apparently Raymer was responsible for organizing the Midwest Art Exhibition at the college that spring and had found himself in the position of accepting mediocre work to avoid hurting the feelings of submitting artists. "I blame myself above all others for the recent failure to at least begin reaching toward a higher goal," he wrote. "I could have forced the issue. I didn't because I wanted so badly to come back next year that I hesitated to create any more of a storm than I did. I followed the line of least resistance." Raymer also told Lindquist that he now regretted preventing a student from writing an editorial in the *Messenger* about the exhibition's deficiencies.[97]

Untitled, Taos landscape ca 1947, watercolor, Raymer Society Collection.

Losing the teaching position at Bethany was a severe blow to Raymer and he struggled to regain his sense of direction throughout the summer of 1947. He had, as he told Lindquist, asked about enrolling in courses at the University of New Mexico, but in mid-May a letter from Raymond Jonson informed him that it was too late in the school year to do so.[98] Jonson sought to be as helpful to Raymer as possible, however. He was also a former student at the School of the Art Institute of Chicago (and one of the city's most prominent young modernist painters until he left in 1924),[99] an old friend of Birger Sandzén,[100] and the judge who had chosen Raymer for the Lorton Gold Medal back in 1937.[101] He suggested, therefore, that Raymer take summer classes at the University's Field School of Art in Taos.[102]

Raymer jumped at the idea of studying in Taos. The northern New Mexico town had been a mecca for artists since the turn of the century and Raymer himself had long dreamed of living and working there. He and Ramona had visited the area together two years earlier,[103] but this time she stayed at home. Instead, Raymer traveled with Milford Greer, a student of his at Bethany, and signed up for the maximum of eight credit hours of course work at the Field School.[104] Both men fell in love with the place. They reported to the *News-Record* that New Mexico's landscapes were "wonderfully provocative of creative work. There the high space and brilliance of sunshine lend a strange intensity to a land steeped in the color of its native Indians and old Spanish settlers. It is a country that calls for expression, a land that drives pictures from a person with the need of telling others of it."[105] Greer was determined to buy a house there with money from his G.I. bill.[106]

With similar thoughts, Raymer suddenly burst out in a letter to Ramona, "We've simply got to have a house out here. We've simply got to!!"[107]

Raymer was also enthusiastic about his new friend Greer. He told Ramona that, next to her, Milford was probably the best companion he could take to Taos.[108] Raymer praised the young artist's work, suggesting that his paintings "fairly sing with color" and reminded him of Van Gogh.[109] Greer was flourishing in the Southwestern environment and doing so well that Raymer began to have some doubts about his own progress by comparison. "The kid is certainly doing a good job of painting N.M. Makes my work look weak along side of it. His drawings are improving in an amazing way too. Wait till you see them. I'll hit my stride one of these days tho."[sic][110] The two of them decided that after returning to Lindsborg they would exhibit the work they had done in Taos. They would also build a craft shop and studio on the Raymer property (the first part of an envisioned "craftscenter"), install a large ceramic kiln, and embark on the making of decorative ceramics.[111]

But all was not well at the Field School. Raymer quickly concluded that the faculty was not challenging, the students unmotivated. Lez L. Haas, the director of the school, "seems sort of windy," said Raymer.[112] He could not tell if the man really meant it when he praised Raymer's efforts, or was "just too lazy to say anything else."[113] The other professors were similarly at fault. Randall Davies praised everybody, Andrew Dasburg was "OK in his generalities on art but weak on individual criticism,"[114] and Ernest Blumenschein raved on so about such insignificant work by other students that Raymer and Greer walked out of the class in protest.[115] As for the students, Raymer thought they were "pitiful" beginners whose informal dress, "jeans and t-shirts," offended him.[116] Worse than that, he thought, "very few of them are here to do any real work. Just play around. Most disgusting."[117] Not a hint of this disappointment appeared, however, in Raymer and Greer's end of the summer report to the folks back home. The instructors at the Field School were now presented as "mature distinguished artists" who brought a "wealth of ideas and sound advice" to their young charges. The students, since they came from all over the nation, created "a situation conducive to healthful comparison and argumentation."[118]

Other anxieties tormented Raymer as well, drawing his mind constantly back to Kansas. Once he arrived in New Mexico he wrote to Ramona admitting that he was "a little scared" about the whole venture.[119]

He frequently told her how homesick he was and that he missed her. "This place isn't good without you," he said plaintively.[120] Raymer and Greer actually held off paying the tuition until classes were well under way, so uncertain were they about remaining in them.[121] Added to this was the lingering bitterness about Bethany College. "If I ever see Emory I'll tell him off," he raged,[122] but since that would not be possible, he took satisfaction in knowing that others had been critical of the way President Lindquist had dealt with him.[123] He persisted in the hope that if Annie Lee Ross, another instructor in the Art Department, did not return after the coming term then perhaps he and Ramona could share the position.[124]

Now that he had no teaching to look forward to, Raymer was anxious to start a new livelihood. "You know we have to make a living some way," he reminded his wife, "and I'd like to know soon if it can be done." They had discussed ceramics as a possible answer and he was impatient about getting the studio in Lindsborg ready for production. While he was in Taos, then, Raymer asked Ramona to learn about glazes, write to supply houses about bisque tiles and plates,[125] and advise him about when to purchase a kiln.[126]

It took years for Raymer's anger about losing his teaching job at Bethany to fade. He had no respect for Charles Rogers' abilities as an artist or teacher. One day early in 1949 he visited the Art Pavilion to look at some student paintings, only to find the "unguided effort of a lot of kids that would be better off in some other department." When Rogers showed him a self-portrait he had recently done, Raymer thought it "as cheap and rediculous [sic] as anything of that sort can ever be." He told Greer:

> "I picked up an art book that was lying about & thumbed through it. I came to a couple of Cezanne things, a still life and one of the bather series. Rogers, looking on, informed me that he had seen the originals in some museum in the East and that he 'didn't get anything out of them.' Boastfully told me that he had spent a whole month in museums during the summer - one would think that something would penetrate - Poor Rogers - Poor Bethany!"[127]

Thus, because he was so unhappy with Bethany's Art Department, Raymer advised young aspiring artists to stay away from the college altogether.[128]

Bethany would disappoint Raymer one more time a few years later. Although he had not pursued graduate study after that summer in Taos, he applied for the vacancy created when Rogers left in 1953.[129] The college turned, however, to John Bashor who had earned his master's degree at the

University of Iowa.[130] Nevertheless, Raymer's animosity toward Bethany eventually dissipated and he became a strong supporter of the town's most important institution of the arts. He frequently showed his work on campus and regularly attended arts events.[131] In 1958 and 1960, he acted as guide and lecturer when Bashor took his students on study trips to Mexico.[132] In 1967, when Bethany's president G. Kenneth Andeen created a furor by suggesting that the institution could ensure its future by moving to Colorado, Raymer claimed, "If the College moved, I would too. There would be nothing left."[133]

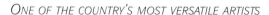

ONE OF THE COUNTRY'S MOST VERSATILE ARTISTS

Birger Sandzén may have had his own studio, next to his house and directly across the street from Bethany's campus, but it was the college that served as the focus of his artistic life. Bethany provided Sandzén with a secure institutional context within which he could develop a career as an artist. Primarily in return for his teaching, the college bestowed upon him a position and paid him a regular salary. This support freed Sandzén from the demands of the art market, allowing him to specialize in the medium and genre of his choice.

Raymer had hoped that he could also combine the roles of artist and teacher in a college setting. Now that Bethany had turned to someone else, he would either have to find another source of steady income or, at much greater risk, attempt a career as an independent studio artist. He chose the latter. Of course, Raymer would be "independent" only in the sense that he would not be part of an institution and obligated to serve its purposes. He would be, in fact, very dependent upon many people to help him make, promote, and purchase his art. He would have to cooperate with others in establishing a network of relationships, an art world of his own that enabled him to do the work he wanted. His world, unlike Sandzén's, would be based in the town of Lindsborg. Raymer also differed from Sandzén because circumstances forced him to become more versatile. His artistic range was naturally wider than the elder artist's, but economic necessity also prevented Raymer from committing his artistic energies solely to painting, which he considered his true calling. Furthermore, to earn a sufficient income he had to distinguish between his art and production work. It was a most uncertain career path.

So uncertain, and thus so unusual, that over the years it became one of the most notable things about Raymer. The Wichita, Kansas, newspaper observed in 1960 that he was "one of the few artists today who is not a

Untitled, still life, oil on canvas, ca1930, class project by Lester Raymer at School of the Art Institute of Chicago, Red Barn Studio.

combination teacher-artist but who actually earns a living creating and selling his works."[134] Decades later Novelene Ross, curator at the Wichita Art Museum, similarly suggested that Raymer's chief significance was that he represented a man "who has devoted himself to the creative life. He has made a living with his artwork. Most artists have to support themselves through teaching. He has refused to participate in the usual routines."[135] Late in his life Raymer acknowledged this important aspect of his reputation and simply said he had been "very lucky."[136]

But along with luck came much hard work and anxiety. Four years after moving to Lindsborg, Raymer knew all too well that there were not many people interested in his chosen art. "Central Kansas is a good place for a painter–if he doesn't have to make a living," he told Clarke Thomas of the *Hutchinson News-Herald*. Raymer was settling down, he contended, in a land of philistines:

Untitled, oil on masonite, 1968, Raymer Society Collection.

> *"An artist needs an audience interested in his creative work to provide the appreciative atmosphere so vital to success. In this part of the country we don't have an appreciative public–let alone a buying public. An artist to live and work must have both. People don't seem to realize a personal need for the enrichment art can give to their lives. The tragedy is that most of them don't know that their lives need more than three square meals."[137]*

If he could not make a living as a painter, perhaps Raymer could transform himself into an artist-craftsman. By producing ceramic objects in large quantity–such things as bowls, cups, plates, and decorative figures–he might earn enough income to support his true art.[138] With this in mind, then, Raymer returned from New Mexico in August 1947 and, aided by Milford Greer and Ramona, set up a kiln and began learning the craft.[139] By the following April, he was ready to introduce Lindsborg to his new creations. He displayed his wares simultaneously in the windows of Anderson's Drug Store, Berggren's Tailor Shop and Gibson's Style Shop.[140] Later in the year, before Greer left for Chicago to continue his studies at the Art Institute, the two men exhibited ceramics at the Red Barn, along with their oil and watercolor paintings.[141] Greer helped to promote the one-day event by writing a letter to the Hutchinson newspaper. He suggested that its readers ought to be interested in Raymer's work: "He is a craftsman and painter who has fashioned a beautiful and unusual home from two barns and filled it with his own craftwork to make of it a tribute to the craftsman's trade."[142]

It was not long before Raymer's reputation as a ceramist began to spread throughout the Midwest. Dudley Crafts Watson, nationally recognized art and music critic from Milwaukee, was so impressed with Raymer's pieces during a visit to the Red Barn that almost immediately afterward he wrote about him to The Haeger Potteries ("World's Largest Art Pottery") in Dundee, Illinois. Watson told Haeger's Vice President, Joseph F. Estes, that he "was absolutely bowled over with the inventive talent and technique of this all-round creative artist." Raymer, he said, was eager to gain a more scientific knowledge about the craft of pottery and might be happy working in the company's laboratory.[143] Raymer, however, had doubts about the move. "Shall I leave here just now when we are slowly but surely becoming known here as craftsmen of worth?" he asked Greer. It had suddenly become difficult to think about abandoning Lindsborg. Raymer was proud that "more people are coming all the time from farther and farther away. Right now they are carrying away things faster than I can produce them."[144]

In the end, though, he never had to make this tough decision. Estes informed Raymer that, while he appreciated his talent, Raymer's designs were far too complex for Haeger's production methods.[145] Those same designs, however, were exactly what Lucy Drage, an interior decorator in Kansas City, Missouri, was looking for. Throughout the early 1950s Drage requested ceramic sculptures from Raymer to sell on consignment at her gallery in Country Club Plaza, the city's posh shopping district. She was especially fond of animal figures such as his unicorns, bulls, centaurs, and horses that sold for $30 to $125.[146]

The chief way for Raymer to generate interest in his work was to exhibit it outside Lindsborg. The annual Decorative Arts Shows at Kansas State College accepted more than half a dozen of his figures, plates, and bowls, along with the work of several other Lindsborg craftspeople.[147] But these may have been the only shows where Raymer presented himself strictly as a ceramist. Between 1944 and 1955, generally the same years he was concentrating on making ceramic objects for local sale, Raymer also attempted to make a name for himself as a painter of regional significance. He selected a small group of his works and entered them in exhibitions held in the larger cities of a six-state area. These exhibitions were, for the most part, annual shows, regionally defined, and highly competitive.

A good illustration of this pattern is the six-year exhibition career of his oil painting *Three Joeys*. In 1944 Raymer entered the work in the Fourth Annual Oklahoma Artists Exhibition at the Philbrook Art Center in Tulsa.[148] Two years

later he submitted it to the *Caller-Times* Exhibition in Corpus Christi, Texas.[149] Denver was the site of the painting's next showing, the Fifty-third Annual Competitive Exhibition of Contemporary Art which was open to artists from 24 western states and held at Chappell House.[150] Then, in 1949, *Three Joeys* appeared both in Omaha at the Joslyn Art Museum's Seventeenth Annual Six States Art Exhibition,[151] and in Topeka at the Mulvane Art Center's Third Annual Exhibition of Oil Painting by Artists of the Missouri Valley.[152] Raymer offered to sell the painting at the Mulvane show for $300, twice the price of another oil he was exhibiting there. A buyer, he no doubt believed, should expect to pay handsomely for a piece awarded a second prize and two honorable mentions and had become his best known work of art.[153]

Certainly one indication of Raymer's rising stock as an artist of merit was the number of invitations he received to present one-man shows. As early as 1950, two members of the Art Department at the Municipal University of Wichita asked him to exhibit his work at their gallery. They had recently visited the Red Barn and admired the "progressive nature" of his art. A display of Raymer's items might "inspire and direct the ideas of our students," they suggested.[154] Raymer transported a total of thirty paintings, ceramic plaques and sculptures, woodcarvings, metalcraft, prints, and even work in a new medium for him, stained glass.[155] Art Department member David E. Bernard thanked Raymer for "one of the more successful (shows) we've had this year," noting also that it had been well attended "by our standards."[156]

The Mulvane Art Center sponsored another particularly important one-man show early in 1955. Again he sent works in a variety of media.

Topekans were very enthusiastic, giving Raymer the most extensive press coverage he had yet received and buying several items as well.[157] Alexander Tillotson, director of the center, praised Raymer as "one of the most sensitive and creatively powerful artists of this region."[158] This high opinion may have been responsible for the Mulvane's purchase of Raymer's wooden sculpture of St. Francis, the piece that the center sent on to Des Moines, Iowa, for an exhibition at the American Federation of Art meeting.[159]

During the early and mid-fifties Raymer strove to keep his art in the public eye. The Kansas Painters Exhibition, sponsored each year by Kansas State Teachers College in Pittsburg, was a particularly good show to enter because it traveled to Wichita and Topeka, Kansas, and Kansas City, Missouri.[160] At Kansas State College in Manhattan, the Friends of Art established a biennial show of Kansas painters in 1950. The Friends purchased Raymer's oil *El Torro*,[161] permitted its reproduction in an issue of *Kansas Magazine*,[162] and a few years later included it in a collection that made the rounds of seven libraries and schools throughout the state.[163] Raymer was a perennial favorite in Hutchinson at the annual Art Association shows.[164] After awarding him a purchase prize in its February 1955 exhibition,[165] the Association asked Raymer to put on a one-man show later in December at the local library.[166] Indeed, 1955 proved to be the culminating year in Raymer's effort to publicize his work. Besides the two shows in Hutchinson there was also the major exhibition of his work at the Mulvane Art Center, soon followed by the Second Air Capital Annual Show at the Wichita Art Museum where his *Wise and Foolish Virgins* received a special merit award.[167]

Admirers were sure that Raymer's work could be associated with some stylistic period in art history; they simply could not agree on which one. They suggested that his paintings, sculptures and craft items were inspired by the Byzantine period,[168] by the "tortured intensity of the Gothic,"[169] or a general "medieval influence working through modern attitudes and techniques."[170] His pieces reminded them of the European baroque,[171] the art of India,[172] and twentieth-century surrealism.[173] But, when the focus shifted to Raymer as artist, and especially to the range of his creative efforts, opinions were unanimous. Throughout his more than four decades in Lindsborg, people described Lester Raymer as a "Renaissance man" because he was so versatile. A 1950 article in *to the Stars* magazine is typical. The author called Raymer "one of the country's most versatile artists," first because he had

Madonna and Child, wood carving, ca1962, Red Barn Studio.

58

St. Francis, wooden sculpture, 1955, purchased by Mulvane Art Center, Topeka, Kansas.

built his own studio/home, and second because his accomplishments in all sorts of artistic media indicated that he possessed "the same varied talent that was a characteristic of such famous artists as Leonardo da Vinci."[174] Ramona once exclaimed: "He's a Renaissance man. He's done it all—the painting, all kinds of sculpture, pottery, ceramics, embroidery, just everything!"[175] Lester later explained that "I can't quite understand any artist doing one simple thing all his life. You'd think he'd be interested in doing something else. I've known artists that can't even use a hammer."[176]

Peggy Greene responded enthusiastically to this versatility. That Raymer worked so well in many materials was a distinct aspect of his "true individuality," well expressed in the 1955 Mulvane show. Greene endorsed the description of Raymer by a friend as an "islander," because he was ingenious, resourceful, and self-confident. She suggested that, while there might be hints of particular historical styles in his work, in the end "he chooses what he likes (and) follows no pattern." Raymer, for Greene, was a man who valued his independence and, therefore, could not be "catalogued." "He needs," she said, "a fresh page of his own." He even refused to live by the clock, varying his work schedule and allowing the spirit to move him.[177]

Greene's feature article for the *Topeka Daily Capital* was a fine example of the journalistic criticism that played a huge role in defining for Raymer's contemporaries who he was and what his art meant. How does one present something so unusual, a full-time professional artist and his art, to an audience as large and diverse as the readers of a city newspaper? Greene approached this problem by emphasizing the artist over the art. She gave her readers biographical anecdotes and career highlights, then shaped them with a theme—individuality—that they could grasp and approve. On the few occasions when she described works of art, Greene was brief and vague, "His design has ease and restraint and he paints with exquisite feeling for color, both in tone and harmony. Human figures are drawn with a soft distortion that seems skeletal and elemental."[178] Her chief interest was not to focus on discrete objects by detailing their aesthetic characteristics and historical associations, but to personalize the works of art by relating them to the artist's life. Greene's statement a decade later that "Whatever he makes bears the unmistakable imprint of his own individuality, a kind of lofty essence of truth,"[179] might stand as the key theme of her writing about Raymer.

Another notable champion of Raymer's art was John P. Simoni, an art professor at the Wichita University who reviewed local exhibitions during the 1960s for the *Wichita Eagle and Beacon*. Simoni believed that Raymer was "foremost among the artists of the state," and yet one senses a certain defensiveness on his part about the fact that Raymer's work remained representational in a time when Midwestern artists were turning increasingly to abstractionism. Simoni felt it necessary to suggest that Raymer understood "art's genuine function of poetic expression," even though he painted "the representational symbol."[180] Raymer had acknowledged abstract art as "undeniably the major trend of our times—or the last fifty years in fact," but he continued to be skeptical about its value, especially its capacity for communicating to the larger public. "Too many abstractionists," he commented in 1949, "have developed a whole system of symbols, meaningless to anyone but the artist himself. Sometimes I wonder if maybe they aren't often meaningless to him, too!"[181] Simoni portrayed Raymer as a serious and sophisticated artist, concerned with formal issues such as color and design, despite his being one of only a few significant painters "who has never abandoned the importance of man's imagery as central motif in art expression." Raymer, Simoni contended, was an imaginative and introspective artist whose human forms expressed "man as actor, performer, or promoter of idea."[182]

60

Of course the buying public responded in its own way to Raymer's art. Many people who purchased his work later felt compelled to express their appreciation in writing. Most common were brief thank-you notes or messages to convey how much they "enjoyed" or "loved" the piece of art they now owned. Often customers revealed their enthusiasm simply by asking Raymer to make some special object or set aside one they had seen during their last visit to the Red Barn.[183] Some wrote to say that they had become Raymer collectors. One person told him, "I feel fortunate that I now own three 'Raymers.' These works, to me, are fascinating; indeed, they provide endless hours of pleasure and are like good friends to be savored and cherished."[184] Others wanted him to know that they were spreading the good word about his art:

> *"I was so delighted with your house and your ceramics, carvings, and other art work that since returning to Lawrence yesterday I have told at least half a dozen people about it. Unfortunately they have not the income to make major purchases at the prices I think you should soon be able to command. I think a few of them are sufficiently interested that they may drive to Lindsborg this fall."[185]*

Every few years or so, Raymer would receive a letter from an especially thoughtful and deeply moved admirer:

> *"I wondered what it is like to be you—if you feel next to God, or if your tremendous productivity and the ease of your genius, has worn down your enthusiasm. I wondered what it feels like when you make things, where does the inspiration come from, is it effortful, what are the costs for you(?)"[186]*

Another customer wrote:

> *"Your paintings touch me. They mean so much to me because they touch me in a deep and quiet place—a place I forget about in the hustle and bustle of everyday life. Every time I look at one of your paintings I am reminded of another side of life and they give me tranquility and strength. …I would like to commend you for the courage and perseverance it has taken to pursue your talent over the years in a world that often tries to measure the value in life through material success and not through beauty, and to thank you for making my life richer through your paintings."[187]*

A MOMENT OF SHARING

Next to Ramona, no one was closer to Raymer, or played a more crucial role in his art world, than Milford Greer. Greer was born and grew up in Geuda Springs, Kansas, a few miles north of the Oklahoma border. When he was fifteen, the family moved to the town of Galva, Kansas, where his father was principal of the local school. Greer enrolled at Kansas State College in Manhattan, Kansas, with the intention of becoming a journalist, but after his freshman year decided to enlist in the U.S. Navy.[188] While he was stationed in Seattle, a "chance conversation" sparked his interest in art. One version of the story has it that the conversation occurred in a department store,[189] another that it took place in the Seattle Art Museum and was with the noted painter Morris Graves.[190] Greer attended painting classes in the evenings before having to ship out on the aircraft carrier *Wasp*.[191] The fall of 1946 found him at Bethany College as a sophomore majoring in art education.[192] Over the next two years, as student and teacher at Bethany, as fellow students in Taos, and then as colleagues at the Red Barn Studio, Greer and Raymer developed a friendship that would endure for a quarter of a century.

Raymer, bitter toward Bethany, no doubt recommended that Greer move on to the School of the Art Institute of Chicago to complete his degree. It must have been painful for him to do so, however. He wanted the best education for his young friend although it would be lonely without him in Lindsborg. His extensive correspondence with Greer over the next few years suggests that Raymer needed to unburden himself to Greer about his early struggle to establish a career as an independent artist/craftsman.

62

The approach of HyllningsFest in October 1948, a celebration that paid tribute to the Swedish pioneer settlers in the Lindsborg region, presented Raymer with perhaps his greatest challenge in that first year of ceramic production. He needed a considerable number and variety of pieces to impress what would be his largest audience to date. Yet early in the month he told Greer he had but ten examples of his work ready to sell. He was feeling "deeply dissatisfied with my way of life here. The hours are so long and yet I have little to show for them."[193] Despite a letter from his friend that helped "to revive these expiring spirits," Raymer admitted to being "a fool full of foolish fears that throw me into periodical tail spins that seem each time to take me lower into the depths of despond."[194] Somehow he found the energy to make a successful showing at the festival.[195] By the end of the month he could tell Greer he was "convinced that with the right location we could make a comfortable living and still have plenty of time left to paint." He looked forward to their eventual partnership.[196]

The next spring Raymer again revealed the heights and depths of his creative spirit to Greer. "About eleven last night I went up to the studio and tore into a painting, in the mood I worked at fever pitch, oblivious of time. What is this thing that drive us thus at times. A torment that can only be quelled by working it out of ones insides."[sic] [197] Six days later his mood had taken a dramatic turn for the worse: "Tonite I am full of doubts—hours and hours spent up in the studio have been fruitless—I'm not sure anymore that I can paint—Like one lost in a forest I go in circles aimless, that bring me back each time to nothing. I need you or someone to talk to tonite."[sic][198] Nevertheless, in his next letter he reported success. "Today I finished what is probably the best painting I ever did and wish you were here to give me your opinion—pro or con—All it took was hours and hours of concentrated work on many paintings, culminating in this one."[199] These swings in fortune and the variations in his temper were a matter of wonder to Raymer. In July of 1950 he declared, "My work—that is my bride, my sword, my crown, my scourge, victory and defeat my prayer, my madness, my crucifixion, and my glory."[200]

In return for Greer's sympathy, Raymer was happy to encourage the continuing student. "I pray & wish with all my being," he once wrote Greer, "that I can take some small part in your struggle and perhaps in some way be able to help you along the way."[201] At times, he could draw specifically on his own experiences at the Art Institute. When Greer complained that Boris Anisfeld was ignoring him, Raymer provided a reassuring context. "Does he ever talk to <u>any</u> of his students? I don't remember that he was ever very articulate with anyone when I worked under him. Even his pets. Used to make me most unhappy and once or twice so mad that I swore that I would never go back to his class."[202] Occasionally, his advice was more general. He cautioned the young man to be patient and to expect that "the 'clearer vision' will come to you. It may be slow in coming and perhaps a very painful process. But that is Life, and the rewards shall make the struggle more than worth while."[203] A year later Raymer gently scolded Greer, "Your painting <u>will</u> improve—Slowly, perhaps, but surely you will come forth—the labor pains will in your case be hard, but there will be rejoicing over the progeny you will bring forth, full of fire, brilliance and strength, worthy of your name and heart."[204] Upon examining some sketches Greer had sent, Raymer paid him the ultimate compliment. "I should be jealous of your growing powers that give every evidence that the day is fast coming when you shall eclipse me, but so far I feel only pride and happiness over the prospect."[205]

Raymer was eager to give material as well as moral support. At the end of the 1948-49 school year, he told Greer that since his own financial situation had been recently "looking up," it was his "fiercest hope" that he could help the younger man pay the bills for one more term in Chicago.[206] When he surprised Greer by sending him a ceramic chalice incised with a line of Chinese poetry, Raymer felt compelled to explain the intensity of his emotions:

> *"Don't be abashed at my generosity Milford. My keenest pleasures come from giving and doing things for those who mean much to me. If the things I give you and the things I do for you give you pleasure and satisfaction then rest assured that I am happy and doubly rewarded in the giving & doing. The hours that I have spent in this last project for you have been happy ones."[207]*

Greer and Raymer shared an interest in other arts besides painting, sculpture, and the crafts. There are references to Degas, Van Gogh, and Lehmbruck in the correspondence,[208] but also to literary greats such as Whitman and Hemingway.[209] Greer once copied a Shakespeare sonnet for his friend.[210] Most prominent, however, is their continuing conversation about music. Greer was an accomplished flutist, and Raymer frequently mentioned how much he enjoyed listening to classical performances on the radio, espe-

*Milford Greer, on left, and
Lester Raymer, 1950s,
Raymer Society Archives.*

cially by the conductor Arturo Toscanini.[211] One November day, while reflecting perhaps on his own struggles as an artist, it struck Raymer how rewarding the great Italian maestro's life must be. He suggested to Greer that " to be able to do something superbly and to be given visible sign of appreciation seems to me to be the ultimate. I think that most people go through life starved for appreciation."[212]

"There is little else that gives me as much pleasure as receiving your words, and little else that gives me as much pleasure as writing words to you."[213] Exchanging letters with Milford Greer was enormously important to Raymer. He believed there was a genuine meeting of the minds between them, a "definite spiritual intercourse."[214] There is an unmistakable sense of desperation in Raymer's portion of the correspondence that suggests he was unable to fully express himself in Lindsborg. Greer, however, offered him a lifeline from Chicago and the larger world of the arts. He was, said Raymer, "an audience of one to whom I unashamedly bare my soul."[215]

Then suddenly, in May 1950, their relationship began to change. Greer informed Raymer that he would not, as he had in the past, be visiting the Red Barn over the summer. That was shocking enough, and yet something bigger was apparently in the works, for Raymer urgently professed his belief in Greer and told him he would see him in Chicago very soon. Even so, he sought to assure Greer that if he were now "only a spectator" in his former student's life, "I shall cheer you on most lustily—as long as there is voice in me."[216]

A year later Greer graduated from the Art Institute with a Master of Fine Arts degree.[217] After a brief visit with his family, he decided that

65

San Francisco might be fertile ground for developing his career as an artist.[218] At first he concentrated on designing stained glass windows. He learned traditional techniques at a commercial studio, and then contributed more contemporary pieces for a projected Buddhist church, whose overall design received a national architecture award. His design for an exhibition of images about hydraulic engineering at the University of California, Berkeley Engineering Department, led to regular employment for seven years with the University's Department of Mineral Technology. He created exhibitions for the Hearst Memorial Mining Building and also slides, brochures, and letterheads for the department. Elsewhere on the campus Greer made designs for the Berkeley Research Center, the Hormone Research Laboratory, and the Museum of Anthropology. On weekends he shared his studio with a life drawing group. He also painted murals for private homes and entered work in group shows at museums in San Francisco and Oakland.[219]

Throughout this period Greer and Raymer remained faithfully in contact with their letters. Greer was constantly encouraging Raymer's effort to build a larger reputation as a painter. He believed his mentor was a woefully under-appreciated artist, but was at a loss to explain why. Yes, Raymer had not devoted himself fully to painting, but Greer admired that "fine balance between work done for a specific purpose and the freer, more personal expression of the work done simply as the expression of one's concepts and feeling." Perhaps Raymer had not been sufficiently aggressive in promoting himself, but Greer admitted that, like his friend, "I lack that particular drive—so hope to achieve results as you do—by doing work of some quality that can be its own advertising."[220] Whatever the reasons for Raymer's obscurity, Greer looked forward to the day when Raymer, "one of America's best painters,"[221] would receive the national acclaim he so richly deserved.[222]

After living in California for about four years Greer, with great apprehension, asked Raymer if it would be possible for him to move back to Lindsborg and work at the Red Barn studio. He sheepishly suggested that he could bring "willing hands and heart " to the venture, but not much money. Nothing came of the idea but, in his attempt to persuade Raymer, Greer eloquently articulated what their friendship had meant to him. Over the years, their relationship had, he thought, "deepened into a kind of permanent awareness of each other." While both men could offer the other stamina and enthusiasm, Greer insisted that Raymer was uniquely encouraging and

had revealed to him "a strength and individuality combined with a warmness of spirit that is ever good."[223]

One bond of friendship between the two men throughout the 1950s was a shared dream of living and working together in Taos, New Mexico. After the summer at the Field School they arranged to meet there at least once, in 1951.[224] Over the next few years, they discussed possible arrangements. Perhaps Greer could move to the area while Raymer used whatever house they bought as an occasional "place of escape."[225] Or, Greer could remain at Berkeley but spend three months each year working on the Taos property.[226] There was even mention of creating a "small community" or "compound,"[227] presumably of artists and craftsmen. Eventually, Raymer said he wanted to stay on permanently in Taos.[228] By 1956, they took on a third partner in their scheme, Dr. Erling Struxness of Hutchinson. For three years, the trio hoped to purchase either a part of the San Geronimo Ranch in Taos owned by the Mingenback family[229] or land belonging to the Mondragon family.[230] Neither plan succeeded.

Finally, in the summer of 1960, the partners bought a house in Ranchos de Taos, about four miles south of Taos.[231] Greer moved in immediately and Raymer visited for a few days the following month.[232] They were excited about making improvements to the building and corresponded frequently about their ideas. A once lofty conversation devoted to their passion for the finer things in life had now become chit chat about furniture, property taxes, and roof repairs.[233] Toward the end of one of these casual communications, Raymer apologized to Greer for sending such a "haphazard collection (of) trivia." Perhaps, he said, he had "lost the knack of writing letters."[234]

After all their efforts, however, Greer occupied the house only eighteen months before offering it for sale with a real estate agency.[235] Apparently the main reason was that the Raymers were unable to move to New Mexico, or even visit for very long. Ramona was uncomfortable among the locals[236] and at 54 Lester was beginning to feel his age, suffering particularly from dermatitis and a possible stomach ulcer. Although his sales figures were healthy, he had not saved enough money to consider building his own house in Taos.[237] Perhaps most important, Raymer was tied down by his many professional commitments. He was at last reaping the benefits of a growing reputation, especially in the field of religious sculpture. In September 1961, he was frantically trying to complete a large commission for St. David's Episcopal Church in Topeka while also preparing for HyllningsFest.[238] Taos remained "uppermost in my thoughts," Raymer told Greer, and yet with all these hindrances he admitted that "maybe the whole idea was meant only to be just a dream. I am wondering if I can take up or find another-"[239]

Milford Greer in North room of the Red Barn Studio, 1950s. Raymer Society archives.

Greer stayed on in New Mexico and within a few years was being touted as "one of the leading young painters of Taos."[240] He exhibited his art throughout the Albuquerque-Santa Fe-Taos region and, like Raymer, succeeded in supporting himself with the sales of his work.[241] He was also a founder, along with Kenneth Schanewerk, a violinist from Texas Christian University, and Chilton Anderson, a local cellist, of the non-profit Taos School of Music. He promoted the school's summer performances by designing posters and brochures.[242] Of course Greer maintained his ties with family living in Moundridge, Kansas, and with his many friends in Lindsborg. On April 3, 1972, he was driving back to Taos after spending the Easter season at home. Suddenly, about thirty miles west of Clayton, New Mexico, the car's axle broke, his vehicle crashed, and Greer was killed. He was 45.[243] There is no record of Raymer's immediate response to the tragic news, but surely he was thinking of the man he called "my most precious & great friend"[244] when he wrote years later:

> *"When you are 80 years old and look back at what your life has meant, you will not focus on your solo activities. What you remember are the incidents of touching, those times when your life was enriched by a moment of sharing with a friend or loved-one. It is our mutual awareness of this miracle called life that allows us to accept our mortality."[245]*

Raymer (left), and Esping in studio with processional crucifix and altar piece for St. Andrews Episcopal Church, in Emporia, Kansas.

THE PRIDE AND TREASURE OF THE CONGREGATION

Subjects drawn from the Christian Bible always played a prominent role in Raymer's art. During the late 1940s and early 1950s, he established his reputation as a painter in Omaha, Denver and other cities with a variety of secular themes, but perhaps even more so with oils such as *Lord Is It I, Luke V:4,5,6,* and *Wise and Foolish Virgins*.[246] His sculptures of St. Francis, both in wood and clay, were very popular with exhibitors and with customers at the Red Barn.[247] When interviewers asked him why he made such things, Raymer bluntly discouraged the notion that he was moved by strong religious convictions. Clarke Thomas noted in 1949 the trend toward religious subject matter in Raymer's art, but Raymer denied there was any reason for it other than that "an artist is always hunting around for suitable subjects and religion gives a wealth of these."[248] Several years later Peggy Greene observed that Raymer painted saints and clowns "with equal gravity and grace." When she asked him about his interest in saints he told her rather evasively that "all artists have a deep religious feeling." Raymer added that he was not concerned with the usual church activities or orthodox religious views.[249] Late in Raymer's career, Elma Byrne of the *Wichita Eagle* quizzed him about the topic and concluded that "he doesn't believe an artist needs to be religious or have religious feelings to execute such work." Raymer advised her, "It's more important to be a good craftsman, to know your business."[250]

Raymer enjoyed great success as a religious artist, regardless of whether he was inspired by faith. The climax of his long career occurred between 1957 and 1965 when national exhibitions of religious art awarded

prizes to his work, and numerous congregations rushed to commission him to beautify their churches with liturgical pieces. Raymer's reputation extended beyond Kansas to include Texas, Michigan, and Illinois.

Early in 1958, the Dallas Museum of Fine Arts invited Raymer to submit examples of his liturgical work for an exhibition called "Religious Art of the Western World."[251] It accepted two pieces, a metal and mosaic altar cross, and a sculpture of the *Madonna and Child,* in metal wire and mosaic.[252] The show was a large one, consisting of nearly 600 objects[253] by masters such as Bellini, El Greco, Cranach, and Goya,[254] as well as by "a few of the nation's best craftsmen" currently at work in the field.[255] *Newsweek* reported that it was "the biggest loan exhibition of religious art ever assembled in the U.S."[256] The director of the museum, Jerry Bywaters, told Raymer that, with over 50,000 visitors during a ten-week run, the exhibition was the most successful the institution had held since its opening in 1936.[257] Both Raymer's cross and sculpture sold quickly[258] and his art received its widest exposure ever.

Another show that requested Raymer's work was the Biennial National Religious Art Exhibition, established by Holy Name Parish in Birmingham, Michigan, and then later sponsored by the Archdiocese of Detroit. In 1960 he entered a metal sculpture, 30 inches in height, of the *Madonna and Child* mounted on a mosaic panel.[259] The sculpture won the Parish's purchase prize[260] and was featured in a photograph distributed nationally to promote the exhibit.[261] *Parade Magazine* praised it and two works by other artists for being "angular and abstract, colorful and contro- versial," thus proving "that church art, like church architecture, has gone modern."[262] But a woman from Pasadena, California, wrote Raymer to inform him that his sculpture proved religious art, "the one true, beautiful Art," could not be made "modern." "Where do you get the idea the Madonna and Child was suffering from malnutrition? This is the most grue- some, not just shocking, work of Art I have seen in many a year. A beautiful figure such as Mary to be made so hideous is sacriligious."[sic][263] Four years later, when Raymer had not submitted anything for the upcoming biennial, the director of the exhibition personally urged him to do so.[264] Raymer decided he would make something even though time was short. During a week of intense effort in the studio, he constructed a crucifix that once again won the purchase prize.[265]

One October day in 1949, Wilfred Hotaling, a young Episcopalian minister from Concordia, Kansas, came to visit at the Red Barn. He had just moved to the region from New York a few months earlier and, because he was very interested in art, decided to drop by and see Raymer's studio.[266] Hotaling discovered to his pleasant surprise that the Lindsborg artist, among his varied projects, also made religious paintings and sculptures.[267] Soon after the visit Raymer wrote Greer to tell him how excited he was about his conver- sation with the minister: "Perhaps (I'm keeping my fingers crossed) he will give me a commission to do three large panels for the altar screen in his church! Is it possible that at last I will get a chance at something like that?"[268] A few weeks later Hotaling did, indeed, inform Raymer that he would contact a possible donor about authorizing him to paint a four-panel reredos. Hotaling thought it important that the church be a discriminating patron of the arts. "It really is criminal when you think how our churches are dominated and ruined

Madonna and Child, wire and mosaic, 1960.
Exhibited in National Religious Art Exhibition, 1960.
Collection unknown.

by people who know nothing of what they are doing. I just wish that I had barrels of money, so I could turn you loose in our little church here."[269]

This combination of admiring church patron and an artist eager to engage in commissioned work would bring Raymer the greatest recognition of his life. For the next several years he designed and executed decorative paintings, mosaics, stained glass, and woodcarvings for churches in north central Kansas.[270] Then, in 1957, Raymer received one of the largest commissions of his career, an assignment to create 24 decorative tiles, two mosaic door panels, a six and one-half foot long reredos cross, a missal stand, candelabra, and vases, all for the chancel of a new chapel at Gloria Dei Evangelical Lutheran Church in Houston, Texas.[271]

Vase for St. David's Episcopal Church, Topeka, Kansas, 1960, designed by Raymer, metalwork by Esping.

For almost a year Raymer was involved in a complex triangular negotiation through the mail with Rev. Elston Flohr, Gloria Dei's pastor and graduate of Bethany College, and Eugene Wukasch, an architect in Austin who specialized in church design. Both Flohr and Wukasch assured Raymer that he was at liberty to design the objects as he wished. They were nearly always happy with the results.[272] Nevertheless, when Raymer submitted sketches for the mosaic panels, they suggested that the one concerning the Resurrection "be somewhat better defined in order to prevent too much of the abstract approach."[273] There were also occasions when cost concerns led them to ask him to modify his original ideas. Flohr, working with a building committee, had to tell him that his proposal for the cross was beyond their means. "Please understand," Flohr wrote, "that we are not trying to get quality art for nothing, but we are interested, perhaps, in simplifying the work as much as possible to get it more within our budget and, at the same time harmonize well with the rest of the work you have done for us."[274] Wukasch expressed a few days later his "regret that it becomes necessary for us to restrict your artistic abilities with such limited budgets."[275] There were also the reminders to Raymer that the church was on a schedule and had to have his pieces by certain deadlines.[276] The experience with Gloria Dei Church showed Raymer that, while commissioned work could be profitable and artistically rewarding, the need to meet the expectations of others also placed limits on one's creative freedom.

Architect Charles Edward Stade knew of Raymer's work in Houston and wanted him to help complete the interior of his latest design, Bethlehem Lutheran Church in Elgin, Illinois. Stade enthusiastically recommended Raymer to Pastor C.F. Wittenstrom, suggesting that the Kansan "could add the final artistic touch and create for you the very best in chancel atmosphere."[277] For three months Raymer toiled on a cross sixteen feet in height and with a transverse that was six feet long.[278] *The Lutheran Companion* remarked upon the conspicuous presence of the huge wooden cross, suspended over the altar and "sheathed completely with heavy copper, except for the center inlaid column, which is of mosaic work and depicts life in Christ through the fruits of the Spirit." The reviewer was awestruck. "Christ has truly marked this sanctuary with His sign," she wrote.[279]

Raymer's third major liturgical commission was located closer to home, at St. David's Episcopal Church in Topeka. Once again, the main piece was a cross for the chancel. The cross was a wrought iron structure, fifteen feet long, with red, blue and gold mosaic tiles, that included a nine foot high bronze figure of Christ the King.[280] Rev. Henry H. Breul, rector of St. David's, proclaimed it a "masterpiece" and told Raymer he thanked God for the artist's skill and insight.[281] Peggy Greene called it "a beautiful piece" and was sure the cross would be "the pride and treasure of the congregation."[282] Photographs and descriptions appeared in *The Living Church* and *Churchman* magazines.[283] The Wichita Liturgical Conference, convened a year after the cross's installation, asked to exhibit a model of it.[284]

Raymer could not have completed the St. David's commission without the assistance of Malcolm Esping, who used Raymer's designs to make the three foot high wrought iron cross and candlesticks.[285] Esping's father was a blacksmith who had emigrated from Sweden. For the son, metalcraft was a second career, following a severe injury in a tractor accident and, two years later, the destruction by fire of his garage and body shop.[286] By 1953, he had opened a studio on Lindsborg's main street and the *News-Record* introduced him as "a new artist on the horizon" who worked in copper, brass, sterling silver, aluminum, and wood.[287]

For some reason Raymer was unhappy with Esping's efforts on the cross and confided to Greer that the metalsmith's "work leaves somewhat to be desired." He also doubted that Esping had the skills needed to execute the candlesticks.[288] It appears that Raymer's frustration with Esping was short-lived, however. During the previous year he frequently used Esping's shop to fashion iron fixtures for the new house in Taos,[289] and was very pleased with a "beautiful" wooden cross Esping had made for him.[290] Later, in 1967, Raymer became the assistant when he made a watercolor drawing

Candle holder and Bible stand, St. David's Episcopal Church, Topeka, Kansas, 1960, designed by Raymer, metalwork by Esping.

73

of Esping's plan for a seven-building historical park complex at the south end of Lindsborg.[291]

Raymer's testiness toward Esping was rooted, perhaps, in a larger preoccupation. Raymer's age and poor health led him to question whether he would ever take on another project as large as the one in Topeka.[292] In the months after installing the cross at St. David's, he suffered with skin and stomach problems[293] and was then stricken by a severe case of strep throat. He told Greer he would look into requests from congregations in Oak Park, Illinois, and Great Bend, Kansas, because he needed the money, but then added "I dread another of these big commissions... All this should have happened 20 years ago."[294] By the summer of 1967 Raymer did quit accepting such assignments. Interviewers discovered a major reason - his aversion to deadlines and any other restrictions on his work.[295] Blunt as usual, he told Dorothy Wood, "I've reached a time in my life when I can do whatever I like."[296] That is, except live in Taos or continue with commissions that brought him wide recognition and considerable financial rewards.

THE SENSE OF SOMETHING SLIPPING AWAY

During the Christmas season of 1965, Peggy Greene decided to visit her friends Lester and Ramona at the Red Barn. Curious about how an artist met the daunting challenge of holiday gift-giving, she found that Lester's versatility served him well. He enjoyed the ability, as the title of her article in the *Topeka Capital-Journal* suggested, to shop "among his talents" by making nativity scenes, angels, candlesticks, wooden fruit and other things for Ramona at Christmas or for her birthday and their wedding anniversary.[297] This was a new perspective on Raymer, a focus not on ceramics, painting or liturgical objects, but on the multitude of small, three-dimensional items he had made over the years and that populated his Lindsborg house and studio.

By December 1969, the press characterized Raymer's annual presents to Ramona as "toys." The *McPherson Sentinel* reported on a wooden monkey on a stick that Raymer admitted was not as "ambitious" as objects he had made in previous years.[298] The monthly issue of *Kansas!*, a promotional magazine published by the state's Department of Economic Development, ran color photographs of a few pieces and noted that the Wichita Art Association would display Ramona's entire collection the following summer.[299] Raymer's reputation as an artist was shifting once again. From now until the end of his life, just over two decades later, the public would know him primarily as a toymaker, an aging artist who made delightfully playful handcrafted gifts for his wife at Christmas time.

Untitled, Handcarved fruit and bowl, gift to Ramona, ca 1950, by Lester Raymer, Raymer Society Collection.

GIFTS OF LOVE

LESTER RAYMER

TOYS ■ TAPESTRIES ■ BOXES ■ PAINTINGS

Brochure for "Gifts of Love" traveling exhibition of Lester Raymer's toys, 1989 - 1990.

The Birger Sandzén Memorial Art Gallery played the key role in promoting public appreciation of Raymer's toys. The gallery frequently exhibited Raymer's paintings, which he insisted were his primary interest.[300] But these paintings changed from show to show, and the circumstances of the exhibitions varied. Sometimes Raymer's art was featured on its own, at other times it appeared with the works of other artists, as in the Midwest Art Exhibition. By contrast, the gallery always displayed the toys at the same time of the year (Christmas), at regular intervals (every two years during the 1980s), and only with other craft items by Raymer himself.[301] This distinctive manner of presenting Raymer may help explain why, for press and public alike, the toymaker overshadowed the painter.

Raymer regarded this turn of events with a mixture of bewilderment and dismay. In 1977, after the Sandzén Gallery had shown the toys for a third time, he cried out to Larry Smith, good friend and long-time correspondent, "I'll probably be remembered as the toymaker of Lindsborg?!!"[302] Three years later, upon the conclusion of yet another show of the toys, he was still a bit mystified by their appeal, suggesting to Smith that such work "seems to attract people-"[303] And when the toys were exhibited as *Gifts of Love* and traveled to Dallas, St. Louis, Oklahoma City, Wichita and other locations,[304] Raymer disclaimed responsibility for the tour and told Smith "I'm not too happy about it!"[305]

Despite the artist's misgivings about his new reputation, the toys were enormously popular. "Everyone is absolutely enthralled by them!" observed Margaret and Pelham Greenough during the Christmas 1980 exhibition. "They just can't believe what they see, that one man had the genius and imagination to create them."[306] Novelene Ross noted that when *Gifts of Love* appeared at the Wichita Art Museum, "some very experienced artists and collectors who came to see that exhibit told me they thought that your work equaled or bettered museum pieces they had seen in Europe. They stayed before the works for a long time and returned several times."[307] One of the thousands of people who would see Raymer's toys over the years wrote him that she was simply "awe-struck" and "overwhelmed" by what she had seen at the Sandzén Gallery:

> *"You never seemed to compromise the art with which you designed each piece for ease, saving of time, or for an average job. Every piece was like its own masterpiece. It was so inspiring to see artwork and truly fine craftsmanship glow from behind the faces of clowns, horses, jack-in-the-boxes, and madonnas. Seeing them was like a visual lesson in the rewards of taking the time and care to do something well."[308]*

Although Raymer had enjoyed a long and fruitful relationship with the Birger Sandzén Memorial Art Gallery, his attitude toward the institution soured considerably during his last years. He complained that the gallery had become a "mausoleum,"[309] a building devoted exclusively to paying tribute to the late Birger Sandzén. He blamed Sandzén's daughter, Margaret Greenough, for the situation, suggesting that she was afraid of any artist competing with her father's reputation.[310] When a collector of Raymer's paintings gave five of them to the gallery, he suspected that they would "just go to the basement and remain there."[311] And yet, it was the Sandzén Gallery that served as the site for a large retrospective of Raymer's art in 1988.[312] Raymer liked the way the show looked[313] and was proud of the large attendance, but still griped that his work could have filled the entire gallery.[314]

Originally the plan had been to hold the retrospective at the Könstverk Gallery, and to make it a celebration of the artist's 80th birthday in 1987. Raymer disapproved of the idea, however, because the art would be on display for less than a week,[315] and, no doubt, because the space was so limited.

North Room, Red Barn studio, 1950s.

Otherwise, the Könstverk served Raymer very well. Each year he was amazed by how much of his art sold at the gallery, and the high prices it commanded.[316] He appreciated the support he received from the proprietors of the Könstverk, Dale Hoag and later, Rick Nelson.[317] Hoag even played the role of "proxy" during a ceremony Raymer said he simply "could not face."[318] In 1984, he was chosen as one of three "Governor's Artists" and had a few of his paintings briefly hung in the Topeka office of Governor John Carlin.[319] The *Lindsborg News-Record* reported that Hoag had accepted the award at the state capital ceremony because Raymer was unable to attend "due to unforeseen circumstances."[320] Years later it was revealed that he stayed home because he had no suit jacket for the occasion and refused to buy one.[321]

This cantankerous side of Raymer was frequently on display in the correspondence he faithfully maintained throughout these years with his old friend Larry Smith. His comments on the weather, local events, mutual friends, and even national politics ("that idiot we have in the White House!")[322] were evidence of an irrepressible urge to observe and assess the world around him. But the letters to Smith are also a record of Raymer's declining body and spirit. Ramona's struggle with cataracts was evidence for him that "old age is Hell!,"[323] her painful arthritis and bursitis proof that "we're both held together only with spit and scotchtape!!"[324] Raymer suffered through physical ailments as well, probably none tougher to accept than the partial loss of his hearing. Soon after turning 71 he sadly concluded it was "no good trying to communicate with most people. Few know how to speak distinctly."[325] In December 1985 he told Smith there was no way he would agree to Ramona's suggestion that they sign up at the local nursing home.[326] Nine months later they placed their names on the waiting list. "We're both deteriorating at an alarming rate," said Raymer.[327]

Lester and Ramona were able to lighten the burdens of advanced age by depending upon Lan Nelson. Nelson was a student at Bethany College when he became intrigued by Raymer's art. He introduced himself to the couple at the Red Barn and a friendship blossomed.[328] In the fall of 1970, the Raymers traveled for six weeks throughout western Europe. Nelson dropped out of school for a semester to serve as their driver.[329] For five years, 1976 to 1981, he lived with the Raymers, becoming a virtual member of the family. His help in maintaining the house, studio and surrounding grounds was indispensable. Along the way Raymer taught him a few craft skills, such

Transom metalwork, created by Raymer for use in the Raymer house, ca 1950, Raymer Society Collection.

as the making of tin stars, decorative items of Mexican inspiration. Nelson would eventually move on to a career as a public school teacher and as activities director at the Bethany nursing home. Nelson remained in close contact with the Raymers until the very end.[330]

By the mid-1980s, Raymer's enthusiasm for work steadily waned and a general weariness of life set in. For a brief time he was stimulated by the intelligence and humor of a new artist in town, Jeffrey Morin, who taught at Bethany for one year.[331] Raymer found in the twenty-six year-old Morin "one of the very few people I ever knew that I could talk to about my work and be understood."[332] But neither Morin, nor the prospect of a grand summation of his distinguished career, could rejuvenate Raymer's once-powerful creative urge. A few months before the retrospective exhibition at the Sandzén Gallery he revealed to Larry Smith how deeply he despaired:

> "Raining here. Been a dark & gloomy day. Matching my mood. One of the days when I wonder what it is all about. What I have not accomplished. What will I do with the remaining time I have?? If there was a way of stepping out of the whole thing, with no pain or hurt for anyone, that would be the thing to do. I think I have been bewitched & I don't know how to handle it."[333]

Photographs from 1988 Raymer Retrospective at the Birger Sandzén Memorial Gallery. Photos from the Birger Sandzén Memorial Gallery Archives.

Left: (l to r) Doris Elliott, John & Judy Bruch, Lester Raymer.

Center: Lester and Ramona.

Right: Dale Hoag and Hilding Jaderborg.

79

During the last months of his life, Raymer kept a journal, a handwritten document of four and one-half pages. The journal is a series of brief and fragmentary meditations on art and life.

"Age brings no pleasures, only compensations, of which the coziest is reading the obituaries of your contemporaries over breakfast."

"The sense of something slipping away, of events obscured by an increasingly opaque veil."

"Death becomes an objective instead of a threat."

"Life is agony and hope, illusions and despair all commingled, but despair outlasts all."

"Life is meaningless—we create certain attitudes which give it a meaning while we exist, though they themselves are meaningless."

"The trivial distractions of daily and nightly existense [sic] with which we obscure the hushed but giant footsteps of our approaching end."[334]

Lester Raymer slipped away June 1, 1991.[335] He will be remembered, as are other artists, primarily by what he made. The curious will look at his paintings, sculptures, and craft objects and marvel at the fusion of heart and mind that fashioned them. In themselves, works of art provide us with only partial evidence for understanding the creative spirit. One must turn to the life from which the art emerged. Raymer can be known through the people he lived and worked with. These individuals and institutions helped him make and exhibit his art, judged its aesthetic qualities, and defined its social meaning. Some even sought to own his art's peculiar magic by purchasing and collecting it. Only by studying Lester Raymer within this art world can one fully comprehend the man behind the art.

...enius is an abstraction which comes to life when its possessor dies. Then his creations start to live, assuming that they have any life at all, for they occupy the place where he stood when he looked at the world, and they offer to those who know how to see it, a vision of what he saw, what he stood for, and what he created for others to look at.

Excerpt from
"The Jester's Shadow," a book
by Jeff Morin, ca 1995.
Illustrations and quotes from
Lester Raymer. Handmade
paper, design and binding by
Jeff Morin.

St. Francis, red clay sculpture,
ca 1950.
On south wall of garage at the
Red Barn Studio.

Thoughts on a Pilgrim Artist

Diane Thomas Lincoln

The whole meaning, importance and value of life are determined by the mystery behind it, by an infinity which cannot be rationalized but can only be expressed in myths and symbols.

Nicolas Berdyaeff

Encountering the mystery behind the life of artist Lester Raymer requires a closer look at his many works of art which focus on Christian symbols and themes. Some understanding of the mystery emerges upon entering Raymer's creative space, the Red Barn Studio in Lindsborg, Kansas. Here he created a kind of personal church, a contemplative hideaway, a beloved hermitage, in which every room and studio surface is touched by his hands and heart. In this delightful environment we see a wide range of the artist's work including sculptures, paintings, and diverse crafts. It can be said of Lester Raymer, who was both highly creative and deeply reflective, that he never settled on any one solution to his work, nor did he compromise his own true interests. Raymer produced an enormous body of work which is captivating, challenging, and nearly always born from a deep spirituality. His works alone are a testimony to his love of creating. And, though Raymer was not an overtly devout man, his art and environment were created out of a deep personal theology.

Raymer's various styles and ways of working merit close examination. One can come to an understanding of the artist and his work by looking beyond the paintings and crafts, going deeper into his visual litany of Christian symbols. Doing so necessitates the acknowledgment that Raymer's work was informed by Christian art traditions and symbolism which point to

Top: Untitled, painted cross, oil on wood, private collection.

Above: Untitled, Madonna and child, 1960, Red Barn Studio.

higher realities. Symbols can never reveal the full extent of the mystery behind the meaning and value of art or the life of which they are a part. But symbols can direct and inform us of the numinous qualities in both. Raymer's work, especially his sacred art, is imbued with this fervent search for what is sacred and holy.

Raymer is important to us in this secular, technological age. The sacred art forms which he built, painted, and sculpted were appropriated from sacred art around the world. These forms now assist viewers in recognizing and celebrating diverse religious cultures, various artistic traditions and stylistic approaches, many of which have virtually disappeared from popular religious culture. In this sense, Raymer was an early multi-cultural visual arts educator. He was personally interested in the relationship between various world religions and bodies of art. In addition to his ever widening study of Western art, he was possessed with a love for Spanish and Byzantine traditions. Raymer was a *santero*, a keeper and carver of the old holy images, a Byzantine copyist monk, and in the broader Christian tradition, a "mystagogue," one who transports the faithful into the realm of the beautiful. Raymer was also a liturgical artist who was commissioned to create ecclesial work for various religious denominations. The commissions which awarded Raymer the most honor were the liturgical arts used in religious ritual and worship.

He maintained the essential symbols and myths of Christianity during a time in which the Industrial Revolution, secularism, and science were replacing religious tradition. With the advent of secularism, mechanical reproductions replaced the aestheticism of practicing artists and the guilds the church had once sustained.

Raymer's own spirituality can be seen in the forms he produced and in the environments he created. The Red Barn Studio became a place where art and life were inseparable, where the artist could examine tradition while forming a new language built upon the old. The Red Barn Studio itself is a metaphor for an explanation of the rise of early Christian arts.

Primitive Christian art was based upon the merging of Mediterranean and Asian cultures existing prior to the birth of Christianity. The forms which emerged from this fusing of cultural ideals and interpretations were highly diversified. One style borrowed by the Christian art tradition is the awakened, wide open, round eyes found in funerary statues in Mesopotamia and throughout ancient Mediterranean cultures. This expression came to signify

Arrangement in center studio with deer mask, St. Francis, (paper maché,) Madonna and child, (wood carving,) by Lester Raymer. Photo by Jim Richardson, 1998.

the awakened spirit, one touched by a higher force. Raymer came to adopt some of these stylistic tendencies in his own portraits and sculpture. Another example is the portrayal of the human form in a pose which signifies grace or holiness; frontal views of the human body with sinuous and rhythmic lines, reminiscent of Byzantine art. Raymer adapted this treatment of the human form in his carved, wooden Madonnas and images of St. Francis of Assisi.

In the beginning of this now-passing millennium, sacred artists accepted the notion of an unspoken, hidden meaning behind the realities of the world. In this secular age, these long-held traditions, myths, rituals, and symbologies no longer speak to people. Artists like Raymer managed to keep these traditions alive even as the larger culture was putting them to rest. Raymer joined that group of artists who worked to preserve sacred art, sometimes within parochial institutions, but mostly in the undercurrents of the commercial art world. In reaction to the Industrial Revolution, there were European artists, like William Morris and later, Eric Gill, who continued to translate the old and the sacred into new works of art. In the Modern period, we see artists as diverse as Henri Matisse, designing the Rose Chapel in France, Marc Chagall, creating stained glass windows depicting biblical stories, and Georges Rouall, fusing images of Christ with the visual idea of the clown (not unlike Raymer). Like many artists before him, Raymer was intensely focused on both the natural world and the world of the imagination. Raymer's spirituality is evident in his work, in moral stories, ideals of beauty, and enduring traditions of sacred art. He was not afraid to repeat the past. Like a universal scholar/artist, he delved into the sacred mysteries and

85

revelations surrounding the life of Jesus of Nazareth and compared them - in a humanist, Italian Renaissance way, to other cultural, and visual traditions.

Raymer studied the decorative and ornamental craft traditions of cultures the world over. His respect for cultural differences and his curiosity led him to ever-new sources of inspiration. By acknowledging contributions of craftspeople worldwide, Raymer opened himself to the foundations of all that is truly holy; the common, the ordinary, the useful, and the practical. He collected artifacts which he used either in his artwork or in the design of the Red Barn Studio. In the studio one can see Lester's and Ramona's collections of hand-painted dishes from Mexico, glassware, ironwork, and other objects. In an old wooden box which Raymer converted into a storage unit for found objects and cultural treasures, we find glass, wood, and ceramic beads from around the world, ancient-looking clay medallions, and small treasures found during his travels or at the many estate sales and auctions he frequented.

In Raymer's library at the Red Barn Studio, we find evidence of his

strong interest in the history of Western painting as well as other visual traditions. *The Book of Tea* by the Japanese craftsman and cultural historian Okokura Kakuzo speaks to East-West understanding concerning 20th-century problems in aesthetics and technology. Other notable books which Raymer valued and which are still in the Red Barn Studio are *Spanish Arts of Latin America, Masks of the Northwest Ivory Coast, North American Indian Art,* and a compendium of arts and crafts entitled *Crafts of the Modern World.* The images of Mexico and the Southwest are major themes in both the artist's work and in his collections of books. Raymer's library contains books on the sacred art and architecture of Taos, Santa Fe, and the Pueblo Indians, several books specific to *santos*, *bultos*, and *retablo* painting, and mosaic and pottery books from the Southwest.

It is worthwhile noting that artists who establish craft communities are often spiritual seekers. At the turn of the century, Eric Gill, as well as other English, Dutch, and German artists, established communities that produced crafts and sacred artifacts in response to Industrialism. During the period of Raymer's life when he was producing mosaic pieces, he often put students and friends to work in his studio. Raymer seems to have enjoyed the notion of an 'arts community spirit' which this type of activity produced.

The sacred was always at the heart of Lester Raymer's imagination. In his writing, *Sacred Art and the Spiritual Life,* the contemplative monk, artist, and author, Thomas Merton, says:

> *Sacred art is theology in line and color, and it speaks to the whole man; to his eyes first of all, but also to his mind and to his heart. A sacred picture or statue, is an artistic symbol of the Christian victory of spirit over flesh. It is a witness to the power of the divine Spirit at work to transfigure the whole of creation and to "recapitulate all things in Christ, restoring all material creation to the spiritual and transforming rule of divine love."*

Christian sacred art is ultimately about this transfiguration and recapitulation. It flows from an artist who, sensitized by faith, can see the process of divine restoration in material creation. He sees the spiritual in the physical. When viewing the body of Raymer's creative outpouring, one begins to see his creations as a map of his own spiritual path. He encounters the sacred in art and life and then translates this into a visual work of art or beautiful craft. His early obsession with drawing from his observations attests to a heightened perception of the sacredness of ordinary life and the objects with which he surrounded Ramona and himself. His still-life paintings and drawings of a simple white egg or fruits serve as a kind of genesis, a beginning not only of Raymer's language of form but of a deeper use of the symbols which followed.

Sacred art, as all art, is primarily about this kind of perception. 'Seeing' and contemplation are components of the spiritual life. 'Seeing' is about the development of one's inner life and how one comes to judge and value the exterior world. It is about seeing unity and simplicity which provides the possibility of transcendence, bringing about new powers of creative vision. Inner visions are born into consciousness out of one's deepest longings. Observing shares a place in the contemplative life, a thoughtful, careful look-ing at inner and outer realities. Most visual artists, if they are true artists, spend their lives in thoughtful contemplation. Raymer did. Most artists are mystics at heart. Raymer was. Mystics sense this unity and attempt to explain their experience, whether it be in song, poetry, or visual forms. Raymer sought this unity in his work and in his own personal life. He strug-gled to balance his relationship to the community and to his and Ramona's families; to become financially secure while allowing time to make art. Once when his brother, John, was ill, Raymer left the studio for several weeks to help care for him. While Raymer was very devoted to his family and did not hesitate to be with them in times like this, he keenly felt the separation from his studio and his work. Raymer became melancholic, as many artists do when separated from their creative endeavors. Raymer wrote:

> My work is my bride, my sword, my crown, my scourge, victory and defeat, my prayer, my madness, my crucifixion, and my glory, some-thing I shall be granted the chance to take up again.

Raymer was a mystagogue, an artist who maintained and passed on the tradition of sacred arts. He was a keeper of symbols, myths, allegories, and narratives upon which our Western, Judeo-Christian civilization is built. Artists like Raymer are visual storytellers of the holy and sacred in life. Sacred artists, no matter what their religious or spiritual calling, gaze upon the great mysteries so that they might enter into them. Out of this entering in, they simultaneously respond and cooperate. They are inspired, and their art flows from this inspiration.

This act of contemplative observation, in which one's senses are awakened, forms the basis for the artistic process. Behind every artistic response there resides the need to make order out of chaos, to establish meaning from earthly and transcendent realities. This creative process reflects the ebbs and flows of the universe, the cycles of birth, death and restoration. It is a part of creation and the creative process. An abundant creative life requires that the artist be highly aware of his or her own inner voice. To follow this inner voice faithfully requires trusting one's own observations and instincts along the road of self-discovery. The creative life is indeed a pilgrimage, a spiritual path. Lester Raymer lived a contemplative, nearly monastic life as a pilgrim artist. He was spiritually informed by many and diverse sources, resulting in a life of continuous artistic activity.

Lester Raymer forged, from the smithy of his artistic soul, a unique and eclectic symbolic visual language. He was particularly attracted to Gothic and Romanesque traditions. Blending this with Oriental and South American/Mexican traditions, Raymer formed his own personal interpretations. Raymer was, above all else, a visual interpreter of sacred stories.

Remarkably, Raymer's outpouring of sacred and liturgical art occurred during a time when secular culture was divorcing itself from long-held artistic traditions based on symbolic art. It was a time when most artists challenged traditional symbolic systems. One exception to that trend was the Liturgical Arts Movement in America and Europe, active from the 1920s through the 1960s. In the secular art world, much of what Raymer held dear had fallen silent or become incongruous, including the long-established relationship between artist and the church (patronage system). When the decorative and ornamental was replaced by the manufactured, artists became the essential repository for sacred myths, symbols, and traditions. Raymer is important because he dedicated himself to the task of keeping these alive through his artistic journey. Nearly all his work has elements of the sacred; his paintings, sculpture, furniture, toys, and liturgical or household objects. Most of his art was guided by his spirituality, drawn from the sacred task of remembering the past.

This recollection of the past was made easier for Raymer because of his association with Helen Gardner at the School of the Art Institute of Chicago. Raymer worked with Gardner as a student assistant when she was preparing the second edition of *Art Through the Ages,* a classic art history reference book.

Gardner's knowledge of art history provided Raymer with material which he merged fancifully into personal interpretations of sacred themes and symbols.

The Swiss psychologist Carl Gustave Jung said that the greatest problem of modern people is that they suffer from "a starvation of symbols." Lester Raymer, on the contrary, was a well-fed man. Symbols furnish one with direct information about the transcendent. Symbols lead one toward a sense of unity, employing a universal, archetypal language. Sacred art is essentially symbolic art which points to higher realities. The art of Raymer reveals symbolic patterns in content and form. He worked with these ideas for years, resulting in a kind of unity summed up in the Red Barn Studio.

Raymers' clown, moon, sun, rooster, banner, and ladder images each have their symbolic counterparts in the history of Christian art. Among the countless other symbols which Raymer utilized in his artwork, it is these which will be discussed in relation to specific Raymer works.

In an early wood engraving, Raymer portrays what appears to be himself dressed as a clown, a fool, a jester, or a harlequin sitting below two elderly, parental figures. These figures appear aged, their fuller, slumping bodies pulled down by earth's gravity. The image of the clown or fool emerges early in time and is associated with one who has obtained spiritual wisdom or who is on the path toward this goal. Christ is sometimes portrayed in the visual arts as the 'fool of compassion.' In ancient history the fool often became the scapegoat for a king. Similarly, Christ became a fool for the Pharisees in

The Holy Family, oil on board, nd, Birger Sandzén Memorial Gallery Collection.

91

their liaison with the Roman officials. Though Raymer did not claim any connection between his frequent use of the clown and the image of Christ, in the long history of the visual arts the two symbols are often synonymous.

Raymer frequented the circus both as a boy and as a man. He made drawings from his observations of the circus in his boyhood home of Alva, Oklahoma, and later in Salina, Kansas. Some of his clown studies came from these visits. Images associated with the Roman circus were the basis for some of the earliest forms of Christian art. Christian iconographers developed new artistic forms for the early church by borrowing themes and ideas from mosaic and mural paintings which depicted Roman gladiators, circus figures and animals. From the first to the third centuries, A. D., these images could be found on the Coliseum and throughout the city of Rome. The circus, or theater in the round, served as a kind of stage for storytelling and is a prevalent symbol in Raymer's work. His fusing of these seemingly paradoxical images was based upon an understanding of these origins of early Christian art.

Historian of symbolism, J.C. Cirlot explains how contrary symbols function: "Symbolism is what might be called a magnetic force, drawing together phenomena which have the same rhythm and allowing them to interchange."

Raymer's search for sacred images gave him a sense of the universality and rhythmical force of symbolism. He had conversations with others about the universality of Christian art and symbolism, particularly, when he talked with Roman Catholic priest and patron, Monsignor Michael Moran of Russell, Kansas. Raymer's visual constructions constitute a working out of magnetic forces and rhythmic dynamics inherent in specific repeated symbols. Some of these symbols became regular sources of creative energy for Raymer.

The moon, present in Raymer's tapestries, banners, and many paintings, is an ancient symbol of the Blessed Mother. From early childhood and throughout his long career, Raymer was devoted to the theme of the Madonna, Mother of God, and the child, Jesus. He must also have known of the moon's relationship to ancient, pagan harvest rituals and how it merged into Christian art, becoming the symbol for Mary, mother of God, mother of us all, and mother of creation. This feminine image has one of the longest standing visual histories of any form in Western art. In certain Raymer paintings, in abstract areas, the wave or movement of the crescent moon, appears. Sometimes it is just a mark which moves rapidly with the flow of fresh paint, other times the stroke forms a perfect crescent shape. In early Christian murals, especially in the catacombs, the recumbent moon represents a small boat or ship and serves as a metaphor for the pilgrim soul's meeting with the "sea of night" or "the dark night of the soul," the mystic's path. Raymer's sculpture of Our Lady of Guadalupe depicts Mary standing on the crescent moon.

In European paintings of the Madonna, the crescent symbol can be seen, especially in the 11th to the 13th centuries. This phase of the moon is a symbol of harvest time. In ancient times, the waxing and waning of the moon symbolized the seasons and their effect on the crops. Raymer, who worked extensively in sewn fabrics during the 1960s, incorporated both the moon and the sun on a narrow vertical banner. These two Christian symbols have historically come together in portrayals of the crucifixion.

Untitled, Our Lady of Guadaloupe, ceramic, nd, Raymer Society Collection, gift from Peter and Irene kennedy.

The sun, a prevalent symbol in Egyptian, Greek and Roman art, came to represent, in Christian art, the spirituality and glory of Christ. As the ultimate life-giving force, the sun becomes a symbol for the resurrection. In ancient times, the relationship between the sun and moon, both rising in the east, symbolize the mother who gives birth and the son (sun) traversing the sky during the course of a day. At day's end, the son dies, falls into the ocean, returning to the mother, who births the son again - a rhythmic cycle of life and death. Death and resurrection, life from decay, is the central focus of the Christian mystery. In the late 1960s, Raymer took these ideas and combined them in a banner made from various fabrics, fancy cording, and jewels. The image is typically Byzantine: frontal, linear, embellished. The piece hangs in the central room of the Red Barn Studio.

Raymer explored these symbols in relation to the rooster not only because of his experience on the farm, but also because of the form itself. A copy of *The Illustrated Book of Poultry* can be found in the Red Barn Studio's library. Raymer used the image of a rooster for its symbolism in reference to sacred forms and images from Christian art history. The cock or rooster is the morning herald of the sun, rising in victory over darkness. The rooster is also a symbol for the guide of souls on a voyage or pilgrimage. It also came to represent St. Peter's denial of Christ in the garden of Gethsemane where the cock crowed three times. Like the sun, the rooster is a symbol of the Resurrection. Raymer, throughout his long career, held this image close to his heart and reproduced it in linoleum blocks, drawings, paintings, felt, clay, iron, glass and wood. On the last day of Raymer's life, the first of June, 1991, Raymer was at his easel, painting a rooster.

Raymer's use of the ladder provides an interesting example of his understanding of an important Christian symbol and how one symbol beckons another. In one of his many Deposition renditions, Raymer paints the entire background aglow with fire reds and burnt oranges. The entire surface is bathed in this light, reminiscent of the mystical Flemish style of painters of the late medieval period. In the foreground of this piece are Joseph of Arimathea, Nicodemus, other saints, Mary and Mary Magdalene. Their faces are horror-stricken. They show all the gestures of mourning as they carry Christ's limp, dead body forward, held high at shoulder level, nearly out of the picture plane. Christ becomes the slain actor of history or, as in the circus, the fallen high wire walker whose heroism begs immortality. In this beautiful painting, there is no middle ground, only an inflamed background with the hint of a ladder reaching up to a nearly invisible cross—a powerful example of Raymer's constellation of symbols.

In several of Raymer's paintings which employ the subject of the circus, we see ladders being carried, standing, or lying flat. In other works, there is

94

a single staff, trellis or pole, which for symbolists represents the idea of the "cosmic marriage" between heaven and earth.

The symbol of the ladder is very common in iconography all over the world. It is a sacred icon of the Pueblo Indians, who use it in the kiva or ceremonial center. It signified the passage between the upper world and the lower world, the connection between the earth and birthplace of the ancestors. In the Old Testament, the patriarch Jacob is said to have seen a seventy-two rung ladder in his dreams, ascending into the clouds. Throughout history, especially in the Middle Ages, the ladder served as a symbol for communication between heaven and earth, as well as a means for angels to pass through the galaxies, making the transition between the mundane and the celestial. The significance of the number of rungs in a ladder is important. Seven rungs in a ladder suggest the seven stages of the mystic's ascent to spiritual awareness or enlightenment. Raymer played with this system of symbolic numerology in several of his works of art.

Another frequent symbol in Raymer's visual language was the fish. This universal symbol represents the basic life form from which all other life emerges. It is a "*Magna Mater*" symbol because it signifies the earth and the birthing process from the sea, an essential factor for life. In Christian symbolism it signifies baptism. The fish has always represented the sacred, but in the primitive Christian era it came to represent the regenerative, transforming life force surging up from a slumbering state. Seemingly, Raymer, too, used this symbol as a way of awakening his own imagination.

One of the crucial, primary symbols is the enclosed garden. Since the beginning of time, the garden has been rich in symbolic imagery. The enclosed garden is a metaphor for the inner soul, the bridal chamber, and the Blessed Mother. Raymer built an actual garden of stone and brick at the

Red Barn Studio. It is, like other medieval gardens, completely enclosed. Raymer carved stone images of St. Francis, fish, mosaics, and two evangelists, and placed them in his garden. It is, in the truest sense, a garden for contemplative retreat.

With Raymer's medievalist eyes, two subjects seem to become a personal chant. He recreates the Blessed Mother and St. Francis of Assisi numerous times and in different media: toys, paintings, liturgical pieces, sculpture, mosaic, and small decoupaged boxes. During the Middle Ages, both saints were venerated widely and were part of the larger intellectual and artistic movement which pilgrimage routes helped to form. This spiritual movement was born out of a new perception of nature, self and community. St. Francis became a representative of the late medieval "new man" who embraces the feminine spirit, a metaphor for inner birth. This metaphor for the "great compassion" is at the core of true spirituality and sacred art, analogous to the Blessed Virgin Mary. Raymer made many extraordinary images of St. Francis of Assisi, who has remained a kind of ecological saint throughout the past 500 years.

Raymer's visual theology can best be seen in his joyfully obsessive use and investigation of the image of Mary, Mother of God (Theotokos). Raymer seems to have based his prototypes on a wide range of traditions, including Eastern, Byzantine, New Mexico Spanish, International Medieval, German, and Flemish. In several of his free-standing sculptures and portable shrines, the figures stand in poses reminiscent of the Oriental Madonna of Mercy, Kuan Yin. She is the lighter side of the great Buddhist goddess of compassion. Raymer created *retablos* of the Madonna in this tradition while following Byzantine rules for painting sacred icons. One such Byzantine-style icon is memorable. It is no taller than four inches and is encased in a small, tooled leather carrying case appropriated from Raymer's treasure trove of found objects. It is a portable icon which resembles the work of Italian iconographer, Duccio di Buoninsegna, fused with the more angular, broken lines of a Russian Byzantine icon of the Theotokos of the same period. It was not uncommon for Raymer to merge styles and prototypes.

The folk tole painting on a dresser, upstairs in the Red Barn Studio, is reminiscent of Raymer's maternal Pennsylvania ancestry. The Pennsylvania German tradition of folk tole painting is also evident in the decoration he used on his wooden, three-dimensional work as well as his Spanish *retablo* paintings.

One of the most powerful of Raymer's pieces is an oil painting of the Manger with the Blessed Mother. In this crèche-like structure we see the wise men surrounding a tall Madonna holding the child Jesus in her arms. She is dressed in deep sky blue, a color long associated with the Madonna. Her body moves wistfully to the side, emphasizing the precious baby in swaddling clothes, tenderly reaching up to touch the face of His mother. The relationship between the Madonna and Child has a long history in Marian art, depicting the human nature Christ took on. In the Byzantine tradition, which Raymer emulated, the notion of the "Mother of Loving Kindness" comes into existence in the late Byzantine and early medieval periods of western Europe.

A striking feature of Raymer's Nativity is the depiction of the stable walls not as straw, but as a white shroud suspended from the barren roof beams on which two white doves perch. The infant Jesus rests against a shred of this sheeting as it descends and joins the white shawl draped over the shoulder of the Madonna. At the bodice of this white shawl is a small white lamb, presaging the death of Christ and his consequent symbol as the Lamb of God, the innocent victim sacrificed to atone for the sins of humanity. The white fabric is all the more striking as it is set against the black and white checkered floor on which the shepherd boys and wise men kneel. St. Joseph is shown behind Mary, peering around her right shoulder to look upon his newborn son. It is a scene of great tenderness and human, familial affection.

The figures in this painting are very Flemish-looking with their oval faces, round cheeks, and transparent white flesh tones. Proportionately, their heads are slightly larger than real life and the eyes even larger, making the nose and mouth appear smaller. Raymer treats the human form and face in as many different styles and traditions as he does the rest of his work. However, it is interesting to note that Raymer used two particular traditions to articulate his notions of the human face. One came from his love of Mexican folk art, especially the dark-toned faces of Spanish New Mexican *santos*, (small wooden carvings of saints). The other came from his studies of Flemish and German gothic gospel narrative portraiture. In some ways these styles are similar. The chin is narrower than normal, making the crown of the head wider and more pronounced. In most sacred art traditions, the eyes are normally wider, fully alert, symbolizing the inner state of an enlightened soul.

In Raymer's many renditions of the Crucifixion and Last Supper, one can see pathos and anguish in the eyes and body gestures. One crucifix,

Untitled, deposition, oil on masonite, nd, Raymer Society Collection.

Untitled, Madonna and child, woodcarving, ca 1940, Red Barn Studio.

which measures approximately four feet high, is made in the manner of the 15th-century German master, Matthias Grunewald. Raymer, taking his cue from the German "internationalist" painters of the period, depicts Christ in a tortured state, replete with the realities of the crucifixion, including streams of blood flowing from his crown and open wound.

The crucifix, however, is not just a copy of the German internationalist style. Raymer fuses more structure into the form, similar to the 13th-century Italian master Giovanni Cimabue. Raymer maintains a connection to earlier Byzantine traditions by portraying the figure of Christ as not entirely realistic but divine through the use of flat, broken angles, irregular shapes, and an emphasis on line. Once again, Raymer moves between two contradictory styles, blending them together into his own rendition.

In addition to the religious themes already mentioned, Raymer, like many artists, became preoccupied with the Last Supper. In one of the smaller Last Supper paintings, we see Jesus and Judas at the front of the table with the bag of 30 pieces of silver. Some of the apostles raise their hands to the heavens in shock and horror, while others look away from the scene in utter disbelief as Jesus points to the bounty given to Judas. Judas clutches the edge of the tablecloth on which the sacred feast will take place. Rather than an assured figure, one sees in this gesture the bereaved, guilt-ridden Judas, hanging from the tree of his own suicide for his betrayal of Christ.

Here again, Raymer fuses two older, and seemingly contradictory traditions into his own unique interpretation of the Last Supper. To appreciate this,

Untitled, The Last Supper, oil on masonite, nd, private collection,

it will be helpful to examine the similarities of those Byzantine and Spanish traditions, so important to Raymer, and contrast them with the European traditions of painting.

In contrast to European realism and its use of linear perspective which builds a space within the painting, the Byzantine tradition rejected linear perspective in favor of inverse perspective which takes the point of observation to the eye of the beholder. In other words, all of nature conforms to and moves toward the observer. The viewer becomes a participant. Byzantine art was primarily liturgical and served the important function of drawing believers into union with the sacred subject in the same way that liturgy draws participants into union with God and the saints.

Byzantine masters, like the New Mexico *santos* carvers, seldom signed their works, and for the most part, remained anonymous. Unlike the European masters whose cult of personality and fame grew, Byzantine artists remained anonymous in the service of the church and God. As in Oriental art traditions, the artist's main objective was to continue the styles and traditions of the past. They were not so much inventors as they were custodians of ancient artistic formulae. Their job was to find an existing prototype and use correct procedures. If they followed the rules carefully, the personality or uniqueness of the individual would shine forth.

Byzantine iconographers and New Mexico *santero* carvers and painters of *retablos* and *bultos* share some common ground. Both rejected the Renaissance models of realism and perspective. The European models were based upon formal, aesthetic notions while the Byzantine and New Mexico models were based upon religious notions. Still, both were influenced by certain European ideas which broke into these systems. Thomas J. Steele,

S.J., in his book *Santos and Saints; The Religious Folk Art of Hispanic New Mexico*, points out another major difference:

> *The Renaissance assumed that the artist had no need to be a good man to do a perfectly good job of depicting a sacred subject; he needed only be a good painter. Whereas in the Greek and Russian culture of the time only a monk was allowed to paint a holy icon, the Renaissance assumed the opposite view.*

Steele suggests that there is much in the tradition of Byzantine and Russian icons that parallels the work of New Mexican *santeros*. Certain customs were observed by both traditions, such as the blessing of materials, fasting by the artists, and recitation of certain prayers. All of this required the artists' fervent belief that the image they were painting or sculpting had the real and actual presence of the divine in the materials. For this reason, paint was often mixed with holy water, or the cottonwood stump blessed before work began. In both the *santeros* and Byzantine traditions, the objects made are considered to be incarnated, that is, fused with the presence of the holy.

Individuality or artistic expression was second to the greater need to adhere faithfully to rules, codes of conduct, and traditions. The artists did not seek self-expression or their own reputation, only the rightness of the work at hand. This was not the case with Renaissance artists. Steele tells us that, in the Renaissance tradition, the work of the copyist was not considered to be art. The West has long emphasized creative genius and the periodic demand for new forms.

In a 1968 interview with the *Wichita Eagle Beacon*, Raymer professed an alignment with the Renaissance tradition: "You don't have to be religious to do religious art. It is more important to be a good craftsman, to know your business." Sometimes, however, what he said of himself and his work did not entirely square with the reality of his situation. His life was filled with contradictions. He was retiring and often reclusive yet, like most artists, he sought the public eye in order to earn money to continue his solitary work. He did not enjoy marketing his art, but was driven by necessity to do so. He would often refuse to sell a work. He frequently made art with no goal in mind except to please himself and reach a closer understanding of his own working methods. Raymer also made objects as a way to contemplate fragments of the past. Because of this, people found Raymer sometimes hospitable and at other times difficult.

Raymer's collected fragments of the past show up in curious places in his preliminary studies, or cartoons. In these collages, drawings, and half-painted works, we see how the artist borrowed architectural scenes from old lithographs or other available prints. He would paste down a facade of an Italian piazza and then lay his figures over the top, drawing or painting in clouds or other forms, literally building a model which he then redrew and painted on canvas or board. Raymer collected all sorts of scrap art to begin ideas to be developed later.

This curious methodology is relevant for two reasons. First, there is an interesting correlation between Raymer's process and the manner of making a *bulto* in the New Mexican tradition. The paucity of art and materials in this impoverished section of what was originally Mexico was remedied by Jesuit priests and traders who traveled along the Santa Fe Trail and through the Sangre de Cristo mountain range. They delivered materials for re-use as sacred art for churches and chapels. Lithographs and reproductions of all types of art were plentiful in the mid 1800s and early 1900s. Inexpensive reproductions were made in Europe and marketed throughout the world. In much the same manner as Raymer, New Mexican *bultos* makers appropriated images and ornamented them with flattened tin cans, bottles, beads, glass and wallpaper scraps, turning the *bultos* into small shrines.

This working method also correlates to the postmodern artist's working process in which segments of images are appropriated from multiple sources, reconstituted in new ways and in various mediums. David Salle and Julian Schnable, two well-known contemporary artists, have employed these methods extensively in their work. Salle cuts out images from popular and traditional Oriental culture and fuses them with drawings and references to contemporary global culture. Schnable does much the same, only he employs painterly methods and mosaic, or porcelain remanents of china plates. The list of contemporary artists working in this way is too numerous to mention here. Suffice it to say, collage has become, since the time of Picasso and Braque, a major means of 20th-century artistic expression.

Raymer as *santero* made diverse works which employed images of angels and saints. Besides his great interest in St. Francis, Raymer painted various works in oil based upon the legends of St. Sebastian, St. Christopher, and the four evangelists - Matthew, Mark, Luke and John. Particularly in his paintings or hagiographies of saints (which he also carved on to trunks, boxes, and

liturgical objects), Raymer revives gospel stories and the myths of martyrs and saints. The artist chose popular biblical stories from the Old and New Testaments such as "Daniel in the Lion's Den," "The Last Supper," "The Apocalypse," "Jacob Wrestling with God," "The Wise and Foolish Virgins," "The Fisher of Men," "The Birth in the Manger," and "Noah's Ark."

Raymer's liturgical art shows his depth, breadth, and talent for sharing Christian stories. Before we look directly at some of his ecclesiastical art, we need to put this work in the context of the growing liturgical movement in America. New possibilities for Raymer and other artists, seeking to make works relating to their Christian interests, were opening up. This trend allowed Lester and Ramona to earn their daily bread.

Beginning in 1928, the Liturgical Art Society of America was established by neo-Gothic architect Ralph Adams Cram. This movement, which was essentially ecumenical, lasted until 1972, growing from an existing European movement. Its purpose, according to Cram, was to "devise ways and means for improving the standards of taste, craftsmanship, and liturgical correctness in the practice of Catholic art in the United States." It was an organization founded and organized by lay people, primarily Roman Catholic intellectuals, historians and artists. Their work and writings appeared in

Untitled, stained glass, nd, private collection.

102

Liturgical Arts, a journal which lasted 40 years under the editorial guidance of Maurice Lavanoux. Fueling this movement was a group lead by Everitt Harman from the east coast. He formed an organization entitled A Benedictine Oblate's Guild of Architects, Artists and Craftsmen. These groups set about to change what they considered to be a degenerating trend in Roman Catholic art which began with the Industrial Revolution. They believed that Roman Catholic art had turned sentimental and vulgar through mass-produced forms in the early part of this century. They were opposed to molds and machine-made art. They believed strongly in the work of human hands thus dignifying the worker-artist. Beginning in 1850, and continuing through the 1920s, many new Christian churches which required inspired ecclesiastical art were built throughout the United States. Though this movement did not come to Raymer's direct attention, it nonetheless opened new opportunities for Catholic and Protestant artists through the many exhibitions and competitions organized throughout the United States, particularly in the 1950s and 1960s. Raymer achieved high recognition for the commissions he was awarded as a result of the liturgical arts reform movement.

Raymer began to display his liturgical and sacred art in competitive exhibitions, beginning at the biennial religious exhibitions in Birmingham, Michigan. In 1960 and 1964 Raymer won awards for his work. He was awarded numerous commissions, including one for his bronze and mosaic *Christus Rex,* for St. David's Episcopal Church in Topeka, Kansas. He did many other commissions during this period of time, including pieces for Bethlehem Lutheran Church in Elgin, Illinois, Gloria Dei Lutheran Church in Houston,

Left: Gloria Dei Evangelical Lutheran Church, Houston, Texas, interior view.

Center: Cross from the Gloria Dei Church.

Above: Untitled, Crucifix, metal and mosaic, ca 1949, private collection.

Texas, and St. Andrew's Episcopal Church in Emporia, Kansas. Parishes in the Roman Catholic Diocese of Salina, Kansas, commissioned Raymer to make several pieces, including the previously discussed large wooden gothic-like painted crucifix for St. Mary's Church in Russell, Kansas, where Monsignor Moran was pastor. In 1969 Raymer exhibited several pieces in the Pampa Fine Arts Association Religious Art show in Texas. A crucifix, a ceramic Virgin and Child, a santo of St. Francis, and a wooden crucifix were all chosen and published in various exhibition catalogs. Other competitive religious art exhibitions in which Raymer participated were held at Marymount College in Salina, Kansas, in 1964, at St. Catherine's College in St. Paul, Minnesota, 1965, and in 1969, a group exhibition of regional art at Kansas State University, where Raymer displayed his oil painting of *Loaves and Fishes.*

Articles and newspaper interviews appeared throughout these years confirming Raymer's place in the ecumenical religious arts movement. Toward the end of the 1960s, however, Raymer withdrew from the mounting pressure and public attention of these exhibitions and retreated further into his own world at the Red Barn Studio.

The liturgical arts movement ended for numerous reasons including the death of Maurice Lavanoux. One reason was the cessation of its primary force, the *Liturgical Arts Journal* which had, for nearly 50 years impacted public religious arts exhibitions and education centers in the United States. This liturgical arts movement has, however, begun to re-emerge in this country and abroad. Beginning in the late 1980s, the visual arts, as they pertain to Christianity, have blossomed into commissions for artists, new galleries, Christian arts journals, associations, and other networks. If Lester Raymer were alive today, he would probably be gratified to see the immense opportunities available to artists working with sacred forms. But he would have shied away from being labeled strictly a "Christian artist" by any art movement or by any one segment of society. He was more interested in a synthesis of sacred forms rather than being a proponent of any one religious system or belief. Given his penchant for hard work and a solitary lifestyle, he would probably avoid any opportunity which would divert his attention from his studies.

Raymer left few formal documents, writings or journals concerning his visual theology. We do know that Raymer often spoke to others about theology and visual arts, and also about political events and social justice issues. Mr. Bill Wilson of Salina, Kansas, has stated that Raymer would often meet with

Monsignor Moran to discuss various issues. Moran was a professor for over 20 years at Marymount College in Salina, Kansas before he moved to Russell.

They were both interested in the writings of Evelyn Waugh, a popular Catholic author of the day. Sitting on the back porch of Father Michael Moran's rectory in Russell, Mr. Wilson reports that "over 40 years ago" he was witness to these discussions which ranged from universal subjects to theology, philosophy, and to the ever increasing interest Raymer had in sacred art. During one occasion, Father Moran and Raymer spent a great deal of time discussing how Christ might have looked. Father Moran, an avid supporter of Raymer, was a kindred spirit, and shared in the pleasurable task of retracing the history of culture, art, and religious subjects. Both were quiet men, filled with deep curiosity and spiritual yearnings.

Spectators and observers of Raymer's work are drawn into this conversation, as well. In this way, Raymer, pilgrim artist, serves as guide. He conducts a pilgrimage into the past to discover new perceptions of the present. He reminds spectators and observers of what has always been holy in the vast assortment of human cultures. These cultures share varied and beautiful artistic and religious traditions and a universal hope for the regeneration of humanity.

The whole purpose of a pilgrimage is to seek one's own true center, the locus of the heart, its unique beat and rhythm. Even in the old definition of the term, being a pilgrim meant that one was seeking a kind of hidden paradise. Raymer's art is a reflection of his interior landscape. If it is true that artists express conflicts in society before they emerge into public consciousness, then Raymer is a bridge between 20th-century culture and spirituality. Raymer, the perennial pilgrim, was on a life-long journey inward to discover his creative self through the making of his art. Raymer was a monk without a formal monastery; his cloister built upon contemplation of the spiritual. He gazed into the depths of profound mysteries found in sacred art traditions. Raymer's artwork in the Red Barn Studio, museums, and private collections continues to be a revelation of these mysteries.

Next page:
Carnival Sienna, oil on
masonite, 1973,
Red Barn Studio.

Themes & Variations:
Paintings, Drawings, Illustrations & Prints of Lester Raymer

Don Weddle

I t is possible to overlook treasures in our midst in the obsessive courting of what's hot in art as opposed to what's not. The painting of Lester Raymer deserves our attention, not because it represents the cutting edge, but because it serves us well emotionally and spiritually. His work shows resistance to the many thrusts that might propel a talented artist into the limelight.

Many of Raymer's paintings have strong ties to Hispanic works from the 17th well into the 20th century. The color and style of Rufino Tamayo, the famed Mexican artist of our time, is present in many of Raymer's still lifes. His fascination with the strength and magnificence of the Italian Renaissance masters is shown in the grand gestures and powerful anatomy of certain figures in his *Enigma* paintings and in some religious works such as *David and Goliath*.

Raymer owes equal homage to the great transitional artist Paul Cezanne and those who followed. DeChirico, Rattner, Rouault, Beckman, Cremonini, Moore, Berman, early Picasso, and others left their mark on him as well.

It would appear that Raymer is caught between the world of the Italian and Spanish painting of the past and the prophets of the 20th century.

He does not turn away from the past nor revolt against traditional understanding. As an artist, Raymer is not a trailblazer, but rather, a marvelous eclectic with roots firmly planted in the art history of Europe and Latin America. His expressive mode emerges through his personal selection from these venues. What he produced exuded an amazing energy, extracted from whichever manner best suited his needs.

Many of Raymer's paintings are spiritual in nature and often presented in a theatrical setting. Whether the theme concerns religion, ethnicity, fantasy, theatre, or a simple still life, it is imbued with dramatic power. He draws us to his vision of life through the mystical aspects of his art. He clings to the feeling that materialism is a vulgar intruder.

These sources of inspiration can be traced to Raymer's early life. His mother read the Bible nightly to the family and books were plentiful in the household. At an early age, Raymer formed a life-long habit of reading both poetry and prose. As he matured, classical music became his constant companion. Instruments from his collection, such as lutes, mandolins, flutes, and horns occasionally appear in his still lifes. He especially liked opera, and enjoyed listening as he worked.

THEATRICAL PAINTING

In painting as well as in other media, Raymer's predilection for the stage and especially the circus and carnival is clear. This fascination with performers—acrobats, tumblers, and jugglers—is a natural outgrowth of child-hood experiences in Oklahoma. Every summer, carnivals and circuses presented shows, and Raymer's memories of those experiences were vivid. This was not simply a passing fancy that might attract the attention of any young boy. Family and friends of the young Raymer recall his penchant for these traveling companies. He often followed them from town to town. Companions in his adult life also tell of attending performances with him. Yearly, the Ringling Brothers Circus would come to Salina, Kansas, and he would spend the entire day there, sketching constantly. Raymer moved back and forth, sketching the animals and the performers. He knew many of the circus people by name, especially the trapeze artists and clowns.

The carnival and the circus, as a motif, should be understood in terms of a popular response by artists of the 1920s. Dore Ashton, in writing about Richard Lindner, said, "When he was young (for instance) it was taken for granted that circuses, variety shows, and street life were effective analogs of society and could be manipulated symbolically by the artist."[1] Ashton's description of these performers gives substance to Raymer's apparent empathy for these maligned souls, perhaps expressing through them his own sense of estrangement.

In *If This Be Not I* (undated), the players seem reticent to being exposed off-stage. Mask in hand, eyes peering at us askant, the attitude is one of disapproval at the invasion of privacy. This mood appears often in Raymer's paintings of theatrical people. The intimacy of such works gives one the feeling of being an intruder. The world of the stage is one thing, but *entracte* is another. The *pierrot* and harlequin, stock players of the *commedia dell'arte*, are usually servants, unfortunate lovers, or victims of pranks. It is obvious that Raymer identified strongly with these symbols of the scorned or unappreciated in society. It is one of his most often used themes. These are pictorial dramas, mysterious and poignant. They give us strong clues to a darker side of Raymer's life. Our response may be feelings of ennui and melancholy. The theatre is the public performance that masks the private emotions of the artist.

Raymer's theatrical motifs were sometimes used to pose spiritual questions as well as societal frustrations. The painting, *Enigma,* for instance, relates to a story depicting God as a puppeteer.[2]

> *Amidst a scaffolding of poles, streamers and cascading drapery, a drama unfolds before our eyes although a mystery remains. Is the drummer rendering a final drum roll? Is the control panel in the upper left really a cross? Is the dominant harlequin figure a portrayal of the Supreme Being?*[3]

There are, however, other paintings that seem to be simply joyful impressions from his dreams of the circus.

> *The Aerialists (1949) is a fine example of a compact, space-filling composition. It depicts performers floating effortlessly. In a magically transparent 'Big Top' reminiscent of Chagall, the figures circle perpetually counter-clockwise over well-trained horses. Herein one senses Raymer making a connection between two of his favorite amusements, toys and the circus. It is as if one could wind up the painting; the music would begin, and the carousel would play on forever.*[4]

Admittedly, this obsession with the circus sometimes tempted him to produce "pot-boilers." Perhaps the themes were so irresistible that they became exercises that he produced as a pastime. Maybe it was a way of putting bread on the table, as they did sell well. His life on the farm taught him concern for practicality and the necessities of existence. If some of his pieces hint at the routine and the commercial, one can at least understand his need for income.

*If This Be Not I,
oil on masonite, 1966-67,
private collection.
Birger Sandzén Memorial
Gallery, Greenough Trust
Collection.*

*The Aerialists, oil on canvas,
1949, Birger Sandzén
Memorial Gallery Collection.
Painting was a gift from the
Raymers to the gallery.*

*David and Goliath, oil on
canvas, 1950, Red Barn Studio.*

*Untitled, Soldiers casting lots
over Christ's robe, oil on
canvas, nd, Red Barn Studio.*

*Descent from the Cross, oil on
canvas, 1951, Birger Sandzén
Memorial Gallery, Greenough
Trust Collection.*

Perhaps we never can fathom the full meaning of Raymer's most ambitious works. Yet we cannot resist conjecture, especially in light of events relating to when they were produced. One unique painting, *Carnival-View of Siena*, was completed in 1972. In the spring of that year, Raymer lost a most special young protégé in a tragic accident. Milford Greer, a very close friend and fellow painter, was killed in an auto wreck as he was travelling back home to Taos after visiting Raymer. The death of this brilliant young (45 year old) man was an immeasurable loss to Raymer. For twenty-six years, they had maintained a steadfast friendship. When together, they painted. When separated, they exchanged long visionary letters, discussing each other's work, current experiences, music, literature, hopes, and dreams. Although we cannot totally document it, this painting seems to be a tribute to the life of this special friend.[5] The original maquette hints more directly at the relationship between Lester and Milford. In this working model there are two figures peering forward from behind the wall, in place of the dolls and scaffolding in the final work. This representation might well be Lester and Milford. In the final version, do the doll figures symbolize these kindred souls struggling through life? As depicted in the great metaphysical art tradition, *Carnival* has a sense of *weltschmerz*, a pervading haplessness or feeling of time standing still. We can only wonder if this is, in truth, a dedication.

Raymer's penchant for the metaphysical/surreal surfaces again and again in his mature work, and ties quite naturally to that spiritual character of his oeuvre. The paintings of Giorgio De Chirico are unquestionably a powerful influence on Lester Raymer. De Chirico's use of irrational combinations of architecture and objects, anxiety and silence, conflicting perspectives, presence and absence, the conscious world and the dream world, create the sense of infinity that Raymer wishes to stage. The painting, *Carnival-View of Siena*, demonstrates this strange dislocation of elements. The unorthodox perspective, combined with various fragments of man's creation invading each other's space, creates a bizarre and disconcerting image.

In numerous Raymer paintings we are confronted with portrayals of melancholy spacious terrain, isolated arcades, pennants, and performers in strangely silent settings. In another untitled painting on a long, vertical panel, a juggler is portrayed in the foreground, hoops in hand, atop a drum. The figure is set on a stage-like platform. Behind this focal point is a deep, open space, and in the distance, Italianesque architecture. In these works it seems Raymer is acknowledging the work of De Chirico, Tanguy, or even the paintings, drawings, and set designs of Eugene Berman.

RELIGIOUS PAINTINGS

Raymer created some of his most compelling religious paintings in the late 1940s through the 1960s. It is also worthy of note that three of his major works from this period and in this area of concentration were executed in different styles and from different eclectic sources. The expressive mode of the devout Catholic artist, Georges Rouault, seems apparent in Raymer's painting of the casting of lots for Christ's robe, *Untitled,* circa 1949. A heavy black linear construction dominates the painting. The compact space-filling design with somber tones of muted reds and bluish-grays owes homage to the great French expressionist. Ominous and fierce in its slashing architectural assembly, it has the structural feel of a powerful, stained glass window.

In the Biblical scene, *David and Goliath,* 1950, the classicist in Raymer harks back to the Italian Renaissance. The graceful, youthful figure of David recalls the sculpture of Verrocchio or, more possibly, Donatello's *David.* His gentle but determined face is without malice. The lean, graceful yet muscular figure towers over the prostrate, gnarled figure of Goliath. This is an elegant work completely satisfying in line, color and composition.

His painting of the Crucifixion, *Descent from the Cross*, is aquiver with a strong nervous energy.

> *The tension is like that of a coiled spring–giving strength and power relevant to each detail of the body and drapery. There is a pulsating treatment to the background that adds to the supercharged feeling of the moment. This is not the blood and gore of a Grunewald, but it is Christ the man, nonetheless. The corpse being lowered from the cross is laced with hot cadmiums that indelibly mark the pain that transpired.[6]*

These three paintings, *The Casting of Lots, David and Goliath,* and *Descent from the Cross,* are excellent examples of Raymer's sensitive depictions of subject. Totally different in style and execution, and dramatically dissimilar in their eclectic sources, these pieces are moving responses to their individual themes.

Although Raymer denied that these works were more than just interesting subjects, other actions and statements were contradictory. Raymer was not an active member of a particular church but his spirituality

Untitled, Fruit and vase still life,
oil on canvas, 1953, Birger
Sandzén Memorial Gallery,
Greenough Trust Collection.

After El Greco, oil on masonite,
nd, Red Barn Studio.

114

Variations on a Spanish Theme,
oil on canvas, 1974,
Raymer Society Collection

can scarcely be questioned. Upon close examination of his work, whether the subject was performers, lonely piazzas, or simple but compelling still lifes, the content is imbued with emotion and spirituality, laden with provocative questions concerning life's mysteries and what lies beyond.

HOMAGE

In his search for answers and meanings beyond explanation, Raymer turned to artists he admired. The great Hispanic art tradition made an indelible impression on Lester Raymer. We can even sense it in many of his works that are not of Spanish or Mexican subject matter. Of all the artists of Spain, El Greco was the one Raymer revered most. Even though this magnificent mannerist was not actually Spanish, he was the foremost mystical painter of the time and region. In the Red Barn Studio there is abundant evidence of Raymer's admiration for "the Greek." One particular painting of St. Sebastian is almost a copy, as from the brush of an assistant, and is rightly titled *Homage to El Greco.* Bound and pierced with arrows, the elongated figure, gazing soulfully skyward at a dramatic "Toledo" sky, is a moving acknowledgement to the master Lester Raymer so adored.

Raymer's nostalgia for the legacy from this part of the world was most emphatically stated in a large piece entitled *Variations on a Spanish Theme,* 1974. Here Raymer paid tribute to the great triumvirate of Goya, Velasquez and El Greco. Toledo is on the distant horizon, against the dark and ominous sky. In the middle ground the curtains are open on a parade with banners, pennants, flags and crosses. The processional includes both soldiers and religious figures. On the left, a cannon is discharging and a skull lies on the ground. On the right in a compact group is a presentation of the *Infanta* and other players in a Velasquez cast. And is that Velasquez himself at the easel? No! Look carefully and you see it is Raymer himself, posing, brush in hand, as the master did in the famous painting of a royal entourage. In the foreground attention is drawn to three large figures; on the left is Goya's Duchess, (also seen in the middle ground). In the center is a noble bullfighter in splendid array, and on the right, peering out at us, is a representation of El Greco, after a self-portrait by the master. This work is an impressive dedication to the tradition about which Raymer felt so strongly. His passion is unashamed and the bond is forever.

116

The artist, Lester Raymer, felt a strong attraction to the Southwest. His travels to Mexico and Spain may have had at least equal impact on him. In an interview with Dr. Greta Swenson,[7] Raymer declared that his trips to Mexico had the strongest influence on his work. It certainly is true that he found ample subject matter in this region. His paintings of matadors, peasant women and children show his fervent passion for these cultures. Roosters, game cocks and chickens appear repeatedly, as well as figures with baskets or bowls of fruit and vegetables, or fish carried on their heads or in their arms. These are people for whom he had great empathy, a modest and unassuming people, living the simple life.

A Raymer still life owned by the Birger Sandzén Memorial Art Gallery in Lindsborg, Kansas, is an example of his fervent passion for Hispanic cultures. Strongly architectonic in structure, it sings with warm Latin color. The orchestration of this handsome easel painting is further complemented by starkly beautiful forms. The elemental spirit of the chair, compote, goblet, food and cloth is unmistakably Mexican in feeling.

The pageant of the bullfight attracted Raymer. His painting, *El Torro,* in the Marianna Kistler Beach Museum of Art collection, Kansas State University, Manhattan, Kansas, is a particularly fine example of the artist's command of drawing and composition. The vigor, the power, the magnificence of the maddened animal is captured through Raymer's dramatic construction. The line is rhythmic and agitated. The force of the beast, his dignity and fierceness recreate for us the high tension of the arena.

Raymer, even in his youth, had a strong yen for the Southwest. Later he bought property in the Taos area and dreamed for years of moving there. His close friend and fellow artist, Milford Greer, spent time at this modest place, and the Raymers visited there occasionally. By the time Raymer could afford to make the move to New Mexico, he was too entrenched in Lindsborg to make the change. In fact, he and his wife seemed to be content with their lives and the New Mexico property was eventually sold. The Raymers, however, continued to make periodic trips to Taos.

In the summer of 1947, Raymer attended a Taos summer field school of the University of New Mexico and painted landscapes, including a watercolor of the famous Ranchos Church. Here he often used watercolor, always strong in line, color and design.

Untitled, Still life, oil on canvas,
nd, Raymer Society Collection.

El Torro, oil on masonite, 1940,
Marianna Kistler Beach Museum of
Art Collection, Manhattan, Kansas.

*Untitled, Still life with bananas
and apples, oil on masonite,
nd, Red Barn Studio.*

*Untitled, Still life with dolls, oil
on masonite, 1972,
Red Barn Studio.*

119

STILL LIFE

Although the cultures of Mexico, Spain, and the southwestern United States had enormous influence on Lester Raymer, he was inspired by yet another source. In the struggle for deeper response to the still life as a motif, Raymer returned often to the Cezannesque motif of fruit, vegetables, bottles, bowls and fabric. In one of Raymer's untitled paintings, the subject matter is simply twelve pieces of fruit and a metal bowl. The solidarity of the forms in rich patches of color is ordered into a beautiful composition. As in other paintings, this too, is presented with a sense of drama: basic materials expressing something beyond the objects themselves. As Matisse said, "The figure is not the expression–the painting is (the expression)."

In the Red Barn Studio, one of the untitled and undated paintings of apples, peaches, and bananas is a less dramatic, more lyrical composition. By tilting the table toward the picture plane, Raymer emphasized the volumes on the flat surface. The dark band at the top of the work helped realize this goal and accentuated the compact space as well. The curved exteriors of the fruit and the grouping created a rhythmic interaction of parts to the whole. The rhythm of shapes was further unified by the color coordination of the total design.

Raymer generally used ordinary objects of simple shapes in his still life paintings. He enjoyed introducing figures, cats and dolls into some scenes. This often resulted in works that seemed other-worldly or at least strange and haunting. One such painting shows a doll figure twice–once on the table, and again, larger than life, close to the picture plane as if the spirit arose from the inert form on the table. This may suggest withdrawal or disassociation from the world, or it may have no meaning at all. Perhaps it is as Böcklin said of his painting, *The Island of the Dead*, "It is simply a picture for dreaming over."

LANDSCAPE

Many of his paintings of figures, (Biblical, theatrical or ethnic) were in landscape settings, usually dramatic. The serene treatment always contributed vital energy to the total effect of the content. When he chose to concentrate solely on the landscape, the results were equally charged. One untitled piece, circa 1945, is a windswept sand dune. It is almost monochromatic, with cascading topography that undulates in restless serpentine movements, full of zig-zagging pulsations of free-form shapes. The sky, earth,

120

and grasses are all in constant motion. Drama again is the word. Elemental forces, one against another, give us a starkly beautiful reminder of the breathtaking power of nature. The view is from Raymer's living quarters above his studio in Oklahoma. It could just as easily be New Mexico, or even Kansas. It doesn't matter. Raymer made us aware of a phenomenon, and in doing so enriched our knowledge of the world.

In yet another landscape, circa 1951, also untitled, he focused on the bleached forms of dead barkless trees. It is a tight composition, compact and space-filling. In this very shallow construction, we are confronted by a tangled configuration of forms—sometimes appearing to be shrouded figures, ghostly animal forms, or bones. The wiry linear treatment adds to the tortured feeling. There is a sense of the chaotic explosive destruction of the battlefield. The movement is violent and unending.

Whatever the subjects—the Old Mill in Lindsborg, the church at Ranchos, a shaded patio—the structure of his landscapes remains always solid. The marriage of line, shape and color are always vigorous and convincing.

PORTRAITS

Raymer's extensive knowledge of the human anatomy was put to good use. For the most part, the figures in his compositions were players on the world's stage. Strangely, when he did produce portraits, they were accurate in likeness and the drawing masterful; however, they generally seemed to be academic in character. This was not always so. The portrait of his good friend, the actor Delos Smith, grandly presents this thespian in the garb and surroundings of a theatrical performer. Also, in Raymer's *Self-Portrait,* 1936, watercolor, one can sense a more intense emotional depiction than in some of his commissioned portraits.

DRAWING AND ILLUSTRATION

It has been said many times by many artists that drawing is the foundation of visual expression. To browse through Raymer's sketches is an extraordinary adventure. It is in the Raymer Society archives that one can best witness this. On file are not only his sketchbooks, but also drawings on scraps of cardboard or whatever was available—from newsprint to notepads, napkins to envelopes, as well as letters. The works include everything from a few sparse lines to little jewels, finished in full color, complete in themselves.

Untitled, view of field from Raymer's studio in Oklahoma, 1940, oil on canvas, Raymer Society Collection.

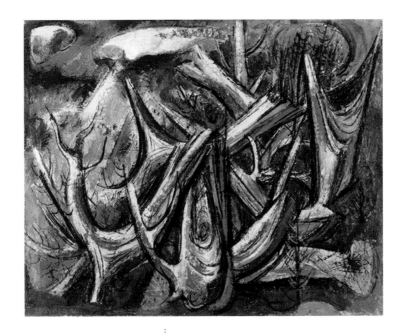

Untitled, driftwood, oil on canvas, 1951, Red Barn Studio.

Self-Portrait, watercolor, 1936,
Red Barn Studio.

1988 photo of Delos Smith in
front of his portrait painted by
Raymer,
Raymer Society Archives.

D. L. Smith, oil on canvas,
1951, Delos Smith Foundation
Collection.

Some of these vibrant drawings are quite abstract, full of vigor and emotion, and exceptional in composition.

"The more you work at something, the more ideas you get," said Raymer. "I have periods when I don't do anything. The only way I can get out of that is to take a pencil, start sketching, and the ideas come."[8] Those closest to him can vouch for the fact that he always seemed to be drawing on whatever surface was available. As with many notable artists, Raymer's draftsmanship is stunning. His merest scribbles seem pregnant with life. Each successive preparatory drawing appears to be larger in concept than the previous one. The intimacy of this process of germination, the birth of an idea, is what excites us.

When Raymer attended the School of the Art Institute of Chicago, the discipline of the classroom and the lessons of the exhibit halls contributed equally to the solid foundation and structure of his education. The strong linear quality of the major part of his work is the natural outgrowth of his drawing. Raymer's immense output of drawing and graphic design while at the Art Institute is solid proof of the rigors of his work there. The subject matter and style of numerous illustrations done as assignments make it plain that Raymer's passion for the theatrical found affirmation in his Chicago studies.

His major painting instructor, Boris Anisfeld, left an enduring impact on Raymer. Anisfeld, a highly accomplished painter and sculptor, will perhaps be best remembered for his sets and costumes for the Russian Ballet, Metropolitan Opera, and Chicago Opera Company. The flavor, sources, and decorative presentation of Raymer's illustrations of Dostoevski's *Crime and Punishment*, prepared as a class assignment, were directly influenced by Anisfeld. Dostoevski's vivid character studies and sympathy for the poor and defeated were subject matter that would continue to engross Raymer.

Dumas's gay, high-spirited, whirlwind adventurers, *The Three Musketeers*, and Stevenson's tale of pirates, buried treasure, and adventure in *Treasure Island*, were two books Raymer loved. His sets of illustrations for the two works are beautiful and strong reminders of his ever present youthful passion for these romantic classics.

Among other literary works he chose to illustrate was Cervante's *Don Quixote*. In retrospect, this work seems totally in sync with the subject Raymer preferred—victims as heroes. The gaunt, simple-minded gentleman, in spite of his jousting at windmills and attacks on herds of sheep, still arouses our feelings of sympathy and, if not admiration, at least our compassion and affection.

Literature was not the only catalyst for Raymer's illustrations. An interest in folk art is seen in many Raymer creations. The last forty-five years of his life spent in Lindsborg left its mark on him. He sporadically toyed with Scandinavian themes, painting furniture, chests, apple trees, and other creations using the peasant/primitive approach of the old Swedish style. His panel paintings in this genre were astounding in the faithful reproduction of this tradition. While, of course, not to be considered original in concept, such pieces gave much pleasure to the community and amused the artist himself. He absorbed this ethnic tradition with the natural ease of a native-born Swede. During numerous *HyllningsFests* he lent his artistic skill to decorating windows and doors downtown.

Recently, a set of eight pieces in full color, depicting the Scandinavian Christmas tradition, were discovered in the studio. They reflect special activities of the season: the sampling of *döpp i gryta,* Christmas porridge, the arrival of family by horse and sleigh, Lucia serving ginger cakes and hot cider to the family, the *Jul Bock,* Christmas goat, delivering gifts, and other memorable occasions.

> *Although he hid it well, Raymer appears to have been a child - at least during the Christmas season. He kept these works to himself in his home, which would indicate Christmas was a private time for him.*[9]

Raymer, at least once, participated in Broadway R.F.D., the annual summer theatre in Lindsborg. He designed a large curtain for the musical, *Oklahoma.* He also created other scenic pieces for this production.

Raymer would, it seems, have been equally at home with another art form as well. While he was a student at the Art Institute, he painted a mural for the cafeteria. Unfortunately, even though this project has been researched, there is no existing evidence of this work. In fact, no photos of the facility have been found. Assuming that he was assigned this project, it is further documentation of Raymer's place of honor as a student at this highly regarded institution.

PRINTMAKING

Although he took a course in etching at the Art Institute, and early in his career produced some woodcuts, Raymer's print work was almost entirely in linoleum cuts. As with so many other techniques, he seemed to have an innate affinity for the medium. He displayed a handsome syntax of varied strokes, rich black and white reversals, and a fine repertoire of textures.

Untitled, One of Lester's illustrations depicting Swedish holiday customs, watercolor, ca 1940, Raymer Society Archives.

Untitled, Illustration from Dostoevski's Crime and Punishment, ca 1935, Raymer Society Archives.

*Untitled, Christmas card,
linocut print on colored
magazine page, nd,
Raymer Society Archives.*

*Untitled, Christmas card,
linocut print on colored
magazine page, nd,
Raymer Society Archives.*

Late in Raymer's life, a fine artist and close friend, Jeffery Morin, selected choice works from Raymer's prints and produced editions on museum quality paper. We owe a debt of gratitude to Professor Morin for this project.

During the waning years of the Great Depression, Raymer produced a set of woodcuts to illustrate the book *Muleshoe Ballads of Oklahoma Bob*, by Marjorie Sawyer Munson. This commission was one of the many ways that Mrs. Munson encouraged the promising young artist. It related directly to three of his loves: illustration, books, and the folk art genre. Mrs. Munson was Raymer's foremost patron and promoter of his early career.

Each Christmas, for many of Raymer's years in Lindsborg, he made Christmas cards–primarily for family. To receive one of these cards was a special treat for many lucky friends. The themes most often used included the Madonna and Child, the Manger Scene, Wisemen, and Shepherds. Raymer often printed these linoleum cuts on colored pages of magazines. They were then trimmed and mounted on paper. The prints were enhanced and personalized, since the effect was so varied due to the variety of colored backgrounds. The style produced the feeling of a stained glass design.

CONCLUDING THOUGHTS

Although Raymer taught painting and drawing at Bethany College for one year, he chose to concentrate solely on his own work. That one year of teaching, though seemingly low key, made an indelible impression on his students. It was 1946 and enrollment was large, made up mostly of veterans. Raymer's work, largely figurative, was a decided departure from the tradition of landscape and still life painting that had long dominated the art department at Bethany. Suddenly all were exposed to Gothic fragments, Italian piazzas, Flemish portraits, Russian icons, classical mythology, private fantasy, and more, much more. His teaching technique was subtle but thought provoking. An evening before the Raymer hearth was a joyful, aesthetic experience, more precious than a classroom could be. Young artists craved his attention, and if they were serious, they got it.

Much of what Lester Raymer produced enlightened the whole community of Lindsborg. Although this small oasis in the heart of Kansas had an art tradition of rather unusual depth, he introduced all to a much broader vista of the culture of the world. The grand array of sketches on his desk, the work in his studio, his collection of treasures, and his interests were catholic in

Untitled, Illustration from "Muleshoe Ballads of Uncle Bob," woodcut, Raymer Society Archives.

Below: Incidental illustration from "Muleshoe Ballads."

nature. Harlequins, peasants, Guadalupes, and gargoyles, plus architectural sketches scattered about his workplace were products of Raymer's fertile mind. Anyone who visits the studio becomes aware of this restless probing into the art heritage of humankind.

Some would say that Raymer spread himself too thin. This may be so. What would he have accomplished had he remained focused on painting rather than working on so many projects—ceramics, tapestry, furniture, toys, stained glass, restoration, masks, muskets, chandeliers, candelabras, sculpture, etc.? What would he have accomplished with brush, pen and pencil if he had concentrated on a more uniquely personal expression? These are questions that cannot be answered. Perhaps what he did was a matter of following his own bliss. We must admit that he left us with fascinating connections to kingdoms not available to most of us. His studio, in some ways, is a cloister-like retreat. He drew on many traditions that leave us with an original and timeless reserve, right here in middle America.

Visually, Raymer was drawn to diverse expressions of the world and its people, to folk art and fable, to symbolism and iconography. It is interesting to see how the different influences mesh or overlap in response to his subjects. Those that are theatrical in setting are metaphysical and religious in spirit. Simple still lifes may exude a Latin flavor, a landscape may be charged with expressionism and performers may be staged amid carnival trappings. Most of his work reveals a poetic soul, with suggestions of subtle nuances, hinting at inner feelings and moods. They become pictorial dramas—mysterious and melancholy.

129

Those of us who respond to the painting of Lester Raymer accept him as an exciting anomaly in the world of art. We identify with his indifference to the culture of the here and now. That is his small rebellion. His use of by-gone styles, his reverence for past traditions, his passion for the simple ways of the peasant artisan and his devotion to childhood experiences have become a way of unifying us and keeping us from being culture-bound in our frantic race toward tomorrow.

As we stroll through Raymer's Red Barn Studio, we become quickly aware of the uniqueness of the experience. The shrewdly crafted icons, the deft works in the manner of El Greco, the homage to Veneziano, recognition of unknown makers of *Santos,* the tribute to Mexican peasants, the admiration for simple Swedish or Polish craftsmen, tell us what we should have known all the while: these are his masters—treasures not to be forgotten. Certainly this is his special legacy. He not only made us sense the poignancy of his allegorical messages, but also brought us to a nexus with our heritage.

On the last day of his life, Lester Raymer worked on two oil paintings. One was of a rooster, strutting across a flat Oklahoma field. It must have satisfied him, since it was signed. The second work, unfinished, was of an angel suspended between the highest cathedral spire and a piercing shaft of golden light.

It seems a fitting closure—a remembrance of his childhood in Oklahoma, and a symbolic sounding of the brass from the world beyond.

Untitled, Rooster, Oil on masonite, 1991, last signed painting by Lester Raymer, Red Barn Studio.

23

The Christmas Toys

Lan Nelson

Note· The numbers beside the photographs correspond to the Toy List on pages154 and 155.

27

Though Lester Raymer would define himself first and foremost as a painter, for many in the public arena he is remembered for the whimsical and brightly colored toys he made for his wife Ramona each Christmas. His work as a toy maker spanned three decades, beginning in the early 1960s and ending with the Christmas of 1990, just prior to his death in 1991.

From oral family accounts, it is known that Raymer made a variety of toys in the mid-thirties. These toys were reflective of the popular juvenile culture of the time. They were made for John and Ellis Raymer, children of Raymer's brother, John. The toys John and Ellis remember included *Pinocchio,* horses, hand puppets, and a rocking horse.

Raymer's tradition of giving his wife handmade Christmas gifts began shortly after their marriage in 1945. These gifts included carved and ceramic nativity sets, wooden and embroidered roosters, imaginative candlesticks, decorated boxes, tapestries and angels, and in 1960, the first toy. It was a clown in a gold and black suit standing in the middle of an elaborately decorated stage—casually lobbing a ball over its head from one hand to the other. It was the first in what was to become a collection of fifty-three carved and costumed toys collectively known as *The Christmas Toys.*

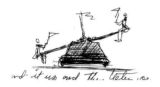

Simply defined, toys are objects we play with; objects meant to amuse or keep us entertained. They are sometimes colorful but often plain–complex in construction, but also as unsophisticated as sticks or clothes-pins lined up in a row, imagined to be a battalion of soldiers marching off to war. Some toys are meant to move, and sometimes the movement is entirely within the imagination of the child lost in the act of play.

A toy "begs" to be handled and explored with eyes and hands: to be captured as it were, by the unfettered imagination. Toys allow us to escape within the inner recesses of ourselves while at the same time playfully inviting us to recreate and re-encounter the world around us. With our toys we discover laughter and embrace life less seriously. With toy in hand we reinvent the definition of joy.

Raymer's toys summon the child within us to handle them, to explore their colors, their forms and their textures: to be inventive, playful and amused. To enjoy. In building toys, Raymer, in the truest sense of the word, 'played' with color, form and texture as well as with movement and drama. Raymer did not consider his toys to be mini-sculptures or serious works of art. As they developed and progressed towards completion, they became gifts of the heart: whimsical expressions of affection, tradition and loyalty. It was time he used wisely to take himself less seriously and also to explore three-dimensionally some of the figures and shapes that played an important role in his two-dimensional paintings. In his toys there are wonderful moments of hilarious movement and expectation. There is both simplicity and complexity in construction as well as encounters with the larger realities of beauty and good design. Making the toys satisfied the playful, more humorous side of Raymer's personality. Working with his hands, carving the figures, fashioning the costumes, and applying strokes of color were aesthetic calisthenics that blended his need to create with the necessity to relax.

Both Raymer and his wife were avid antique collectors from the beginning of their marriage. Over the years, the contents of their house reflected a passion for the unusual, the beautiful and the old. Ramona, in particular, had a fascination for antique toys. She was, however, rarely able to purchase antique toys at auction because of the high prices they always brought. It was out of this desire to own a collection of old toys, coupled with the availability of an empty china cupboard (in need of a collection), that Raymer first conceived the notion to build Ramona the collection she couldn't acquire in the traditional way.

The toys Raymer created vary in size, shape, and color. Primarily crafted of wood and fabric, the collection also contains toys that have metal body parts, figures with composition heads, hands and feet as well as toys which are partially paper, papier maché, and cardboard. The key of one wind-up toy is plastic, an unusual exception.

The early toys, those made before 1970, have colors that are slightly bolder and more defined. There appears to be a less deliberate attempt by Raymer to "antique" the toys through artificial aging techniques, liberally employed after 1970. The color red is used extensively in both early and later toys, but is less dominant in the early pieces. In the earlier toys more color combinations are used. An individual toy might contain as many as twelve different colors.

In the first toys the moving parts were usually handmade, start to finish. Their functions were simple and generally reliable. Changes in humidity and temperature have caused the toys to "swell" and dry out, and consequently to malfunction. A few of the later toys incorporate wind-up clockwork type mechanisms and other parts retrieved from commercially produced toys.

As Raymer matured in his toy building, he became more willing to "borrow" parts from existing store-purchased toys. In some cases he not only re-made, but used the entire toy, as in the *Squeeze Clown Doll with Red Boots* which appears to have started out as an English "bobby." In *Tumbler* of 1985, Raymer took an existing ladder-toy, repainted it, added brass beads as finials and recarved the figure. The *Bell Ringing Clown* of 1983 was built around a composition/papier-maché clown head picked up at a flea market in Wichita one Sunday. *Two Clowns on a Teeter Totter* (1986) uses a wind-up mechanism salvaged from a 1960s Walt Disney cartoon character toy, and the *Red Jacketed Walrus's* metal body first served another toy found in the city of Amsterdam and mailed by a friend to Raymer. The *Clown on the Blue Trapeze Bar* (1975) utilizes the bar and weight balancing mechanism of a prior toy but has a new base and hand carved figure.

After 1970, Raymer incorporates more ornamentation and becomes less concerned with the accuracy of applied paint. Color has been brushed on quickly, with less concern for a clean line at borders or between color patterns. More metal details such as tin cone shaped pieces of metal and four pointed tin stars have been added. All of Raymer's toys are adorned

39

with cloth costumes of various weaves, textures, patterns and hues.

As in his paintings, drawings and prints, Raymer's toys use recurring symbols, design elements and colors that tie them closely together, making it easy for the viewer to identify them without needing to locate his signature. Clown figures dominate. There are no obvious female players, except for Eve in the *Adam and Eve* toy which was made prior to 1970. Raymer's figures are either male or genderless.

Costumes are colorful and rich in pattern and accent details. Gold interplays with red and blue, olive green with yellow. Some of the costumes are solid color, others mostly prints, while in others he combines prints and stripes. Delicate bits of old lace, linen, cotton and upholstery scraps are found throughout in many of the costumes. He put wide ruffled collars on most of his costumed figurines and unraveled the edges of a few of these collars to make them more frilly and airy. There is a common theatrical thread that runs through all of Raymer's costumed figures. The costumes become as important as the figures they cover

1

in setting the stage and engaging the audience in the business of play. There is no poverty, no lack of amusement in Raymer's figures. There is instead a sense of anticipation and expectation.

In all of Raymer's toy characters an active passiveness, a suspended animation is waiting to be awakened, like performers temporarily robbed of motion by the camera's quick eye. In a trance, Raymer's clowns gaze dreamily, not directly toward the audience, but just beyond. The eyes, set in mask-like faces are solemn, heavy and pensive. There is a hint of a smile waiting to appear. Noses are prominent and distinctive, and hats are as important as the heads they cover. Hands are either open, holding something, or gesturing, always drawing the viewer's attention to some pending movement, some serious playfulness.

The ideas for Raymer's toys come from a variety of sources: from books on toys found in his personal library, from commercially manufactured tin toy designs, from folk traditions in America and other countries, from Bible stories, from literary as well as political history sources, from the expressed wishes of his wife, from childhood memories of the circus, and from his own fertile imagination. Raymer would be the first to admit that few, if any, of his toy creations were the result of a purely original idea on his part. What is truly and uniquely Raymer is the lavish manner in which he adorns his toys with color, costuming and sculptural detail. With his skill as a master woodcarver and resourceful craftsman, he successfully combined the world of play with the reality of art, giving the toys his personal signature.

Cyrano de Bergerac, one of the larger early toys, is built around the character of Cyrano from the French heroic comedy of Edmond Rostand (1897). In Rostand's comedy the main character is reluctant to speak for himself in matters of love and longing. The obvious and exaggerated protrusion of his nose is a comical but sorry sight to both himself and others. He is insecure in expressing how he truly feels to his beloved Roxanne. Cyrano uses another to speak to her of his true desires. Raymer, in keeping with the story, uses us to speak for Cyrano, to pull the string that moves his mouth, nods his head, and waves his hands in emphasis or exasperation.

George Washington, Ramona's favorite, is designed after a popular American toy idea, the colonial whirligig. Made for the Christmas of 1968, the main body of the toy stands in a fixed position while the arms are made to rotate in windmill fashion. Holding an American flag in each hand the arms are positioned for balance and visual appeal as well as for maximum exposure to wind movements. The lettering on *George Washington's* base is printed using both upper and lower case letters, just as a colonial printer might have done if he did not have all the same size lettering in his printing box.

Raymer's *Clown in a Chariot Pulled by a Mule* has similarities to the popular Lehmann tin toy "balky mule," patented in 1897. Invented by Ernst Paul Lehmann of Brandenburg, Germany, it was made for over forty years and was widely available for purchase throughout the United States. Raymer was aware of this toy as it began to appear in publications advertising antique toys. Raymer's clown rises from his seat as the reins are pulled back, causing the mule to rear into a kicking position.

The story of Adam and Eve has been told over and over again in the work of folk artists and toy makers for centuries. In Raymer's interpretation of this pivotal Biblical event, Adam looks over his shoulder as he flees from Eve who pursues him, apple in hand. The supporting cast of animals, trees and small plants remains stationary as the two chase each other in a never ending circle. *Adam and Eve* is one of two toys made almost entirely of wood without any metal or cloth detailing.

Another Biblical story from which Raymer draws inspiration is that of Noah's Ark. From this familiar narrative come two toys, the smaller and earliest of the two was made sometime in the early 1960s. In this one Noah and his three sons peer from the end windows of the boat's upper deck, while eight animals bob up and down—their heads protruding from other doors and windows. Just over eight inches in length, it is, like *Adam and Eve,* made entirely of wood. The later Noah's Ark, started in July of 1982 and finished just days before Christmas that year, contains 109 individually carved animals that can be stored within the ark itself or displayed alongside. The ark measures 27 inches stern to bow, and is 19 inches tall. The roof, made of wood and corrugated cardboard, can be lifted off to expose the chest-like storage area within. Although Raymer chose to follow the story by making pairs of all the animals, he carved only one bald eagle. When asked why, his answer was typically simple,"I just got tired."

Raymer's *Monkey on a Stick* (1969) is fashioned after a very early folk toy which may have originated in central Europe, taken subsequently to England around 1800. The book *Toys* by Patrick Murray (1968), from which Raymer took his design, credits the acrobatic construction to Bohemian origin.

"My toys were shown at the Gallery Dec. & Jan. Seems to attract people – Made two new ones this year the clown juggler- ht. 15" – clown tosses ball from hand to hand over head..."

Letter written by Raymer, 1981.

"Gallery" refers to Birger Sandzén Memorial Gallery.

45

53

138

Known originally as a "squirrel," the figures were not always squirrels but monkeys and other animals and figures as well.

The idea for the two *Ladder Walking* toys made in 1985 and 1986 also originated from the *Toys* book. A photograph on page 71 titled "Klettermax" (Ladder Max) provided the initial spark which fired the imagination for these two toys. In this particular toy a figure tumbles down the ladder rung by rung, hopefully landing upright at the bottom. Although the original creation and date of this 'king of toys' is not known, it is likely that it is of relatively modern, and possibly German, origin. Raymer named the first of his two "ladder toys," *Tumbler.*

One Christmas in the early to mid-1980s, Lester's gift to Ramona was a recreation of a favorite Victorian toy called a "Sandtoy Leotard." Invented by J. Leotard in 1859, the magic of this early automated toy lay within. The inner mechanism caused the toy to perform mysterious and graceful acrobatic movements. The toy consisted of a simple, tightly enclosed box on the side of which hung a dangling, loosely-jointed figure. By turning the box clockwise, silver sand is rotated up from the bottom of the box to the top where it begins to trickle slowly down,

funneling over a "water mill" type mechanism. The acrobatic figure's hands are fastened to the bar that juts out of the box from this wheel mechanism. As the wheel turns under the cascading weight of the silver sand, so does the attached bar–creating the illusion that the acrobat is lifting and somersault-ing himself through the air. Raymer's sandbox toy is probably more elabo-rate than the earlier Victorian toys as his comes complete with stage, balcony railing and drawn curtains.

Rodney Peppes' book, *Moving Toys* (1980), provided Raymer with ideas for the two *Military Drummer Boys,* fashioned after *Handwound Drummer* on page 38, and the sitting *Bell Ringing Clown,* designed after *Musical Clown Bell Toy* on page 57. In *Bell Ringing Clown* (1983) Raymer faithfully replicated the mechanism by which the clown's body, arms, legs and head are moved, activated by finger pedals fastened with rope or wire. As an arm or leg is raised–or the head nods, a bell rings. However, with the nearly identical *Military Drummer Boys* (1983), Raymer has simplified the original hand-wound mechanism, as shown in the book, by attaching the back of each drummer's arm directly to a lever installed below the arm and partially concealed in the base.

The idea for the *Cymbal Playing Clown* (1977) appears to have been taken from the book An *Illustrated History of Toys* by Karl Fritzsch and Manfred Bachmann (1965). Color Plate #2 shows a red costumed harlequin with a full lacy white collar and a face with a half-amused, sleepy expression. He has a large red nose accented by reddish high-lighted cheek bones. In his hands he holds a pair of brass cymbals. From the photograph in Fritzsch and Bachmann's book, it is hard to decipher just what mechanism is used to set the clown's arms in motion. In Raymer's version the movement is achieved by squeezing the upper torso of the body. This causes the upper arms to move inward, pulling the arms and hands toward the center of the body. The arms, hinged at the elbows, cause the cymbals to strike. The German-designed harlequin holds carefully shaped and hammered miniature cymbals, while Raymer's clown plays cymbals fashioned out of tin lids from small juice or tomato paste cans. Raymer's figure has an intensely focused countenance, a real musician's seriousness and devotion to the music he is about to make.

Folk toys often embody the strong ethnic traditions of those who crafted them. Borrowing from a few of these traditions, Raymer has replicated at least two Polish folk toys and one familiar, traditionally German plaything.

140

Sometime in the early 1950s, probably prior to 1953, Raymer became acquainted with the Polish *szopka,* a small Polish Christmas puppet theater modeled after the architectural form of a church. It was carried through the streets of Poland at Christmas time by carolers who stopped and acted out the nativity. Raymer designed and built his own version of a *szopka,* mostly of wood, accented by beads, gold leaf and figures fashioned from local clays. Though made before 1960, and exhibited alongside the other toys in the Sandzēn Gallery Christmas exhibits, Raymer never considered this nativity construction to be one of the collection of Christmas Toys.

47

For the Christmas of 1990, Raymer crafted his final toy for Ramona. It was also fashioned after a Polish folk toy that Raymer had. Six horses pull a brightly painted four wheel cart, with the two lead horses slightly larger than the others, standing side by side. The other four horses follow each other nose to tail, going round and round on a carousel that rotates as the toy is pushed or pulled. The original Polish toy is crudely carved and has little color applied. Raymer's cart is colored as richly as a circus wagon. The horses are smooth and highly stylized, painted like Swedish Dala horses. The influence of the Swedish Dala horse in the carving and painting of many of Raymer's horses was a direct result of the strong Swedish folk design traditions he encountered in Lindsborg.

The German tradition of a "turning pyramid" was the source for Raymer's three-tiered revolving nativity set which dates from the middle 1980s. The original "turning pyramids" rotated as wind currents turned the blades of a horizontally positioned windmill mechanism above the pyramid. Raymer simplified his pyramid variation, replacing the windmill mechanism with a manually turned knob. On the bottom level, Raymer has his wisemen arriving in Bethlehem on horseback rather than by camel–probably more of a Swedish tradition than German. Joseph, Mary and the Christ child, along with an assortment of animals, fill up the second tier, while four angels herald the new birth from the top of the third and final tier. Curiously there are no shepherds found anywhere in this toy, due most likely to space limitations.

Raymer has crafted several of the toys in this collection from childhood circus and carnival memories. His giant *Ferris Wheel* (1988) has four male passengers all waving triangular shaped flags. The *Merry-Go-Round,* housed on a square base under a tent-like canopy, has four elaborately carved galloping horses bobbing up and down as the carousel turns to the rhythm of the revolving, hand activated movement. The *Clown in a Cart* struggles to hold the reins

5

of a kicking donkey while the *Lone Aerialist* hangs passively, grasping a bar—ready to perform acrobatic stunts at the squeeze of a hand.

Raymer's clowns pop out of boxes or throw balls from hand to hand. Two figures perform a child's playtime ritual of teeter-tottering, while another with orange yarn hair and a big bottom sways back and forth to a simple nudge of the fingers. He puts an oversized clown in the seat of a tricycle and another on a push car and then, almost with tongue-in-cheek, he artfully combines an American circus wagon, Swedish horses and a cage of chickens on their way to the market, and makes them all part of the same comic scene.

Although the majority of Raymer's toys appear complex in their construction, detailed in design, and rich in color, they are all constructed of ordinary materials and miscellaneous discards one might find in a wood-working shop or at the bottom of a sewing or jewelry box. Most of the toys have been crafted from wood, with additions of cloth, metal, paint and other items such as beads, lace and braiding added as finishing touches.

Most of the wooden parts of the toys were carved from soft pine; the smaller appendages such as heads, hands or feet were carved from a single piece of wood. The torso of the figure, legs, arms or base, were often shaped

142

27

4

7

48

46   50

from a rough block of several pieces of wood laminated together. Raymer would whittle with a pocket or butcher knife, sometimes shaping the figure with a meat cleaver or a small hand miter saw. The finer work was done with wood rasps and occasionally a dental drill. Finishing up with sandpaper, he prepared the figures for paint and costumes. In addition to pine, other woods such as walnut, maple and cottonwood were used in the toys. Even tree roots were a source of carving material from time to time. At least one of the toy horses, however, is not of wood but of papier maché, "reworked" through the application of many fresh layers of paint.

Because most of the toys are small to medium in size, nails were rarely used in their construction. When needed, Raymer used dowel rods to connect sections of the toys so that the structure would be more sturdy. He used small amounts of wood putty or filler to conceal gaps or other unevenly joined surfaces. He often mixed acrylic or other water base paints with the wood filler to make it blend in with the finished painted surface. Many of Raymer's stationary toys have a supporting base or platform. Others are on wheels, allowing the toy to be rolled.

From start to finish Raymer used what was at hand in the design, construction and finishing of his toys. He approached the construction of his toys like he approached all other areas of his creative life—with a frugality and resourcefulness where nothing was wasted. He would combine, invent, and make do, recycling old parts into new aesthetic combinations. A cart with wheels purchased at a farm sale was incorporated into the 1983 *Clown and Donkey Cart* toy. *Nested Blocks,* which once had belonged to Ramona's niece, were repainted and decoupaged with old copies of paintings and art prints. A stray feather from a pillow or duster became the plume in Cyrano de Bergerac's hat. Small round-headed brass nails or pearl beads fastened with straight pins became buttons on a clown's jacket. Coiled picture wire tethers a bird to the cap of a man who reaches up over his head trying to prevent its escape. Can lids became musical instruments; a bristly pipe cleaner, a monkey's tail; and a nearly expired eraser became a ball, tossed back and forth through the air. The *Roly Poly Clown* was formed over a foam ball using papier maché.

Raymer used ordinary sequins to outline and strengthen design elements in the saddles of carousel horses. He incorporated disassembled jewelry pieces and cheap five-and-dime craft materials. Detail was added to costumed figures using embroidery floss, braided roping, lace tatting and old crocheted remnants. He fashioned thin copper sheeting into flags, toothpicks into flag poles, a common upholstery tack into a belt buckle, and used nylon fishing line to provide hidden tension for the movement behind the aerialist's acrobatic stunts. For the body of his "lumbering" *Red-Jacketed Walrus* (1976) he used old flannel bags once used to protect silver from tarnishing. Old silver Christmas tinsel was turned into hair for angels on the *Angel Carousel* (1985). Pieces of marbleized paper from the end pages of an antique book were decoupaged onto the sides of the base of one toy while clipped landscape scenes and alphabet letters were used to decorate the sides of two of his three *Jack-in-the-Boxes* (1971). Raymer cut up wooden cigar boxes to make the sliding doors of his 1982 *Noah's Ark*. The springs used in his *Jack-in-the-Boxes* were retrieved from the local dump, and an old red plaid umbrella canopy became the pants and jacket of the *Cymbal Playing Clown*.

With few exceptions, Raymer's toys are designed to require some initial manipulation or lightly applied motion. Some of the toys need only a simple push to make them work. The *Clown on the 3-Wheel Wagon, Clown Driving a Donkey Cart* and the *Rooster on Wheels* are examples of what can be classified as "push toys." With a push across the table or floor the clown rises up from his cart seat while his donkey rears back. With a push the clown on the 3-wheel wagon wildly pedals the front wheel of his wagon and raises his baton slightly, and the rooster struts up and down in place, his head nodding, his tail feathers and wings rising and falling to the rolling movement of the platform on which he stands.

Pulling a string, a pair of ropes or a wire activates the playful antics of seven of Raymer's toys. With a gentle downward tug on a string, a pair of angels float gently downward, their wings lifting and falling for several seconds. The *Juggling Clown* (1960) tosses a ball from his right hand to his left and back again when one places a finger into the ring and wire attached below the toy and tugs lightly downward, each tug being the catalyst for another throw of the ball. The *Drummer in White Costume* (1963) strikes his instrument through the same applied motion.

Cyrano's strings-and-rings system makes it possible to control five separate arm and head movements simply by pulling the correct string from below the toy's box framework. A pair of clowns, each holding ropes in their

"Toy – turn the suspended circle until the cord is wound around the upright pole. Release & it winds down & back up and down on its own steam - goes on for some time - each turn getting shorter etc."

Letter written by Raymer, 1986.

145

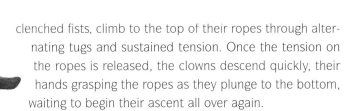

clenched fists, climb to the top of their ropes through alter-
nating tugs and sustained tension. Once the tension on
the ropes is released, the clowns descend quickly, their
hands grasping the ropes as they plunge to the bottom,
waiting to begin their ascent all over again.

Other toys have to be cranked to set them in motion.
Turning a lever on the side of the base causes the *Clown
with a Bird on His Head* to raise his hands up and down
above his head trying to catch the bird before it flies away.
Cranking a red wire handle on the base of another toy
allows two clowns, seemingly slightly inebriated, to bob
up and down and slightly bow. Raymer's *Ferris Wheel* is
another toy which has to be cranked in order for movement to take place.

The acrobatic *Monkey on a Stick* moves with an up
and down sliding action. One pole to which the monkey's
arms are fastened is held stationary while a second pole
to which his feet are attached slides up and down the
shaft of the first pole, making the monkey appear to do

38   36   51

147

handsprings and somersaults. A squeeze to the mid-section of the *Cymbal Playing Clown* makes his arms bend inward and brings the hands and cymbals crashing together. A quick unlatching of a hook releases three *Jack in the Boxes,* and pressing any of the five wooden pedal levers of the *Bell Ringing Clown* triggers his "musical" action.

Three toys spin. With a downward stroke of a finger, *George Washington's* arms spin vertically. By winding the platform of the *Angel Carousel* either clockwise or counterclockwise and releasing it, the angels begin spinning horizontally. Raymer's last toy combines both pushing and spinning motions. As the *Carousel Pull Toy with Six Horses* (1990) is pushed along on the table, the two lead horses remain in fixed positions while a small carousel of four horses on the back spin round and round. The larger *Four Horse Carousel* and *Turning Nativity Pyramid* have knobs that must be turned to make them revolve, while the *Roly-Poly Clown* is rocked into motion when the torso is touched.

The *Red Jacketed Walrus, Two Clowns on a Teeter-Totter,* and *Clown on the Blue Trapeze Bar* move automatically through built-in, commercially produced wind-up mechanisms. The two *Ladder Toys* are dependent on proper positioning of the figures at the top of the ladder and gravity for them to work.

Lastly, there are Raymer's stationary toys, the ones that require no pushing, pulling, cranking or winding for enjoyment to take place. Raymer's Polish style *Szopka,* his *Stacking Blocks* and various clown figures or dolls are mostly visual and require only minimal handling.

A few of the toys—some by happy coincidence and some by design and careful planning—produce not only motion but sound, further enhancing the appeal of the toy. The figure in the *Clown with Bird on its Head,* rises slightly up on its "toes" with each upward crank of the handle. As the handle is turned downward the arms reach upwards toward the head as if to attempt to catch and prevent the bird from taking flight. In between these two standing and reaching motions an ever so slight "chirping" sound is produced. Looking at the toy's exposed mechanism, it is not obvious whether Raymer planned this particular sound effect or if it happened by chance. Raymer did admit, on at least one occasion, that the sound this toy produced came about purely by accident. Raymer did, however, design the "clop" in the gallop of his *Military Man on a Galloping Gray Horse* toy and the flat, monotonous "thud" of the drum roll of his pair of *Military Drummer* toys.

148

The Bell Ringing Clown, on the other hand, is constructed with military-like precision to ring five small bells attached to its arms, legs and head. A pressing motion on pedal keys at the front of the toy's base controls the action and the musical sounds of the bells. From the beginning, Raymer intended this toy to move and make sound. With a firm squeeze to the mid-section of the *Cymbal Player,* a pair of can-lid cymbals "clank" together and produce a sound that is more dull than bright, more percussive than musical. Process rather than outcome, motion rather than quality of sound seems to have been the motivating factor for Raymer in this particular toy. Then there is the *George Washington Whirlygig* that produces a creaking, wooden windmill sound, not necessarily intentional, as the arms are turned by either mechanical or natural wind forces.

Did Raymer intend the casual observer to find hidden symbolism in his toy creations? Was it Raymer's conscious effort to instill meaning beyond the obvious enjoyment and visual pleasure he built into each of his toys, or the enjoyment one feels interacting with them? Why are there so many horses? Why is the color red so dominant? And why do the gazes of his clowns have a trance-like quality, inviting the viewer just so far into the world of the artist? We might wonder as we consider that red has always been the color identified with "vibrancy of life," courage, youth, love, and creative power. Or that red is the color of the soil of the land on which he was raised, that horses have been used to symbolize intellect and speed, and roosters throughout art history are representative of watchfulness and resurrection! Do the instruments Raymer places into the hands of his jesters signify joy? Are the mask-like faces on his figures masking a childhood that was hopeful and promising, simple and uncomplicated—or one troubled with adult-like cares and responsibilities?

Playfully, Raymer has infused drama and anticipation into every toy. He has used rich costuming, perhaps solely for visual effect but also perhaps to conceal shabbiness or to enhance the ordinary. He has skillfully "sharpened" the noses of his characters, made their mouths strong, angular and tightly drawn. The cheeks are flushed with color on one toy while the next appears pale and ghost-like. Are the toys the product of and therefore symbolic of, a richly imaginative memory fashioned in childhood: a memory capable of refashioning in minute detail—in toy form, as well as in two dimensional painting—all the wonderful sights of a traveling circus or an

20

28   *30*   *29*

Oklahoma farmstead? What symbolism, if any, is there to be discovered? Is it important to explore this particular genre of Raymer's creative genius?

If there is any symbolism to be found within the whole of Raymer's toy-making experience, perhaps it is not to be found so much within the parts or components which make up individual toys as in the wholeness of the collection: the expression of Raymer's creative genius and gift for preserving—in an artful fashion—a bit of the child in all of us. The toys themselves elevate play to an art form. Childhood is represented as a beautiful and fragile collection of experiences that are not so much to be seized, manipulated and controlled, as they are experiences to be desired and reverenced, beheld and viewed with a detached but inquisitive curiosity.

Though produced over a thirty year period from 1960 to 1990, Raymer's toys have had, for the most part, a limited viewing audience centered around the Lindsborg community. Visitors to the Red Barn Studio have occasionally been given a glimpse of the toys when Ramona invited them into the house where the majority of the toys were displayed year-round.

Creche, ca 1950,
Raymer Society Collection.

11

12

13

The living room, kitchen and back bedroom all had assigned nooks or hooks where the toys could be seen as well as played with. Rarely did Ramona rearrange the location of the toys.

For many years, during the Christmas season, on a once every two to three year basis, the Birger Sandzén Memorial Gallery in Lindsborg hosted the toy collection in the south exhibition room, at that time called the Green Room. It was during those one and two month Christmas exhibitions that Raymer's reputation as a toy-maker began to take root and, at times, eclipse his already established recognition as a painter. Thanks to regular visits by classes of Soderstrom Elementary School in Lindsborg, fascination with Lester Raymer as a master toy-builder began to grow and provide motivation to Lester as well as Ramona to carry on this yearly Christmas toy-making tradition.

It was in 1989 and 1990 that the toy collection left Lindsborg for the first time when a major traveling retrospective of Raymer's work titled "Gifts of Love" was organized. Sponsored by Exhibits USA, a sizable portion of the toy collection traveled throughout the Midwest. Over a thirteen month period the toys, along with tapestries, boxes and paintings, were exhibited at six regional public art museums in Kansas, Oklahoma, Missouri and Texas. The exhibition received a warm and enthusiastic reception wherever it was shown.

Raymer was often asked, "How long did it take to make this toy or that toy?" It was a question that would sometimes annoy him and at other times amuse him. The answer was always "not very long!" He often waited until two or three weeks before Christmas to begin, and then would work sometimes night and day to get it done on time. Working on the toy allowed him an excuse to sit in front of the television in the evening without feeling he was wasting his time. He often thought he spent way too much time making each year's toy. A particular mechanical problem might take several days for him to figure out so that the toy would work just right. Often when the toy didn't work exactly as he intended, he would move on to worrying more about how the toy looked–its design and use of color–than how it worked.

He fashioned the toys in a limited work area in front of the TV, on his lap, or at his cluttered studio work table. Though he spent hours building the toys, he spent minutes wrapping them, if at all. Often the wrapping would be the previous Sunday newspaper's comic section and the toy would arrive under the tree just in time for the gift exchange Christmas morning.

There were no rules as to the number of toys Raymer would make for his wife Ramona each Christmas. It was always at least one, but it could be as many as three or even four, as it was in 1982.

The "magic" ended in December of 1990 as the last toy was finished a few days before Christmas. It worked perfectly and, in Raymer's mind, there would not be another toy until next Christmas. On June l, 1991, whatever idea Raymer may have been entertaining for that year's Christmas gift to Ramona died with him.

He wrote some about the toys to friends and family, but kept most of their secrets safely locked away in his imagination until they became, for him and us, a creative reality.

Raymer built the toy collection Ramona had always dreamed of owning. He shaped the characters and the movements as well as the sounds that brought each toy momentarily to life. How he really felt about what he had created—sometimes out of nothing more than scraps and left over paints and discards—we cannot positively know. What is apparent, without question, is that each year's toy gave enormous pleasure to the creative process that was alive and well in Lester Raymer.

43   31

3

Lester Raymer's Christmas Toy List

19

21

15

22

1	1960	Juggling Clown
2	1963	Drummer in White Costume
3	1963	Circus Wagon With Cage of Chickens
4	1963	Small Noah's Ark
5	1968	George Washington Whirligig
6	1969	Monkey on a Stick
7	Pre 1970	Stacking Blocks
8	Pre 1970	Clown in Chariot Cart Pulled by a Mule
9	Pre 1970	Adam and Eve
10	Pre 1970	Clown with a Bird on its Head
11	1971	Small Jack-in-the-Box
12	1971	Medium Jack-in-the-Box
13	1971	Large Jack-in-the-Box
14	1972	Pair of Staggering Clowns
15	1972	Man on a Railroad Push Cart
16	1973	Horse on Red Base
17	1974	Horse on Blue Base
18	1976	Clown on the Blue Trapeze Bar
19	1976	Red Jacketed Walrus
20	1977	Cymbal Playing Clown
21	1979	Military Man on a Galloping Gray Horse
22	1980	Napoleon Style French Juggling Clown
23	1980	Rooster on Cart with Wheels
24	1981	Small Acrobat
25	1982	Medium Acrobat
26	1982	Large Acrobat
27	1982	Large Noah's Ark
28	1983	Military Drummer Boy 1
29	1983	Military Drummer Boy 2
30	1983	Bell Ringing Clown

25

32

8

33

34

49

31

*Three other toys have recently
been identified in private
collections, but are not
included in this essay.*

44

Jan 6, 1970

156

157

Transformations

Carla Scott, PhD.

I ndividuals transform their own environment to conform with their creative souls, collecting symbols to express the passion. Sometimes these transformations are self-directed; other times they are the product of one's life. Making sense of one's perceptions and expressing them through visual mediums is an essential part of the soul of an artist. Lester Raymer transformed everything in his life, enriching the artistic spirit within.

THE RED BARN STUDIO BEGINNINGS

Lester and Ramona, from 1947 on, were busy creating the legacy of the Red Barn Studio. Raymer worked in Lindsborg at the Red Barn Studio in much the same way as he worked in Oklahoma. He focused on painting and drawing while developing his talents in a variety of other mediums. Raymer was seldom idle. On visits, he would doodle. If he watched TV, he would do stitchery or create tin ornaments. If he was in the studio, there were always numerous projects in process. Raymer expresses his approach; "I'm in the midst of a new piece of work, sort of lose myself in it hours on end." "I sure wished I had some extra hands." "As I have probably said many times before there just aren't enough hours in the day."

Top: Large, slip cast glazed rooster, ca 1950.

Above: Unglazed red clay wall piece, ca 1960, Red Barn Studio.

159

Lester and Ramona in front of original home, now the north side of the Red Barn Studio. 1947 photo from Ramona's scrapbook.

APR. 17, 1947

A visitor to the Red Barn Studio in 1973 wrote to thank Raymer for the visit and concluded his note, "I have grown up with art, but for me, there is something miraculous about the way you take ordinary materials and give them new life." Many individuals labeled him as a master craftsman with a sense of design and technical mastery. Raymer seemed to have a natural affinity for all types of materials. He had an uncanny ability to assimilate foreign elements and materials into his style. It became a lifelong trait of Raymer's to search out the ordinary and transform it into the extraordinary.

MATERIALS FOR TRANSFORMATIONS

Both Lester and Ramona Raymer enjoyed going to auctions and yard sales. Lester collected things from these sales for his artwork. He also collected things from individuals in the community by trading or sharing. Dale Hoag brought masonite floor underlayment to Raymer. He painted on these boards, which may explain why Raymer's paintings often have odd measurements. Sometimes friends would knock on the studio door to deliver boxes full of unwanted or broken items. Later, these things would show up as a beautiful part of one of Raymer's projects.

When Raymer wrote to his friends, he often requested such things as sketch books and catalogs. He would ask about sources for materials such as gold leaf and colored glass. Milford Greer, in response to such a request, made arrangements for a fellow Art Institute student to travel through Kansas to assist Raymer with ideas related to stained glass. Raymer frequently sent money to his friends, both Greer and Larry Smith, acknowledging receipt of painting and drawing supplies.

Another collector of "stuff" in Lindsborg was Leo Opat, a friend to Lester Raymer and Malcom Esping. Opat would listen to Raymer talking about a new project, look through his own treasures, and bring back items for the new project. Opat's wood became the base for the St. Andrews crucifix in Emporia, which Raymer made with Esping's assistance.

Anytime something was being torn down Raymer would explore the options for retrieving materials. When Raymer had his studio in Oklahoma, he

160

actually worked with demolition crews in several locations in Colorado. He was able to obtain many "choice" items through this work. In Lindsborg, Raymer continued to seek out demolition sites to procure special items. An artist friend, George Boles, remembers going with Raymer to Salina, Ellsworth, McPherson and other locations to get scraps from demolition sites. He would also assist with tearing down a home to obtain spindles and other such items. Raymer utilized these spindles in several cabinets, railings and wall dividers in the Red Barn Studio. Clearing out the south studio storage area after Raymer's death yielded a stash of 102 boxes full of spindles of all sorts and sizes plus a variety of lumber and architectural ornament and trim pieces.

Boxes of leftover ceramic bathroom tile obtained from friends were treasured for mosaics. Fabric and fabric trims used in Raymer's banners and toys were throw-away samples from Shirley Schmidt's Morton Interiors in Hutchinson, Kansas, and from Dwight Putnam's interior design business in Salina, Kansas. Raymer gleaned a variety of materials from the Brunswick Hotel including boxes of samples left by salesmen which had been stored in the upper level of the hotel.

Raymer frequented Ronald Galler's scrap iron business in Hutchinson, Kansas. Galler worried about who this person was that was spending so much

Untitled, clay rhino sculpture, ca 1950, Birger Sandzén Memorial Gallery collection.

time out in the scrap yard. Finally Galler asked Raymer to stop by the office and visit with him. Raymer explained to Galler that he was an artist and that he created art objects with the materials he was finding in the scrap yard. Galler suggested that Raymer bring some of his art for him to see. Maybe a trade could be made. When Raymer finally brought the artwork to the Galler's home, a business deal was started which both parties long enjoyed.

Howe's Lumber Yard in Lindsborg was a regular stop for Raymer in his continual search for materials. Don Howe was the owner of the lumber yard at that time. Raymer would forage through the scrap piles of lumber and other materials. Don Howe's son, Brad, remembers how Raymer would sometimes make things appear to be scraps or leftovers so that he could bargain a price for them. Mismatched custom mixed paints from Howe's became paint for the studio.

RAMONA RAYMER'S ROLE

Soon after the Red Barn Studio became a reality, Ramona Raymer focused her life on promoting Lester's artwork and assisting him with the business of the studio. She cleaned the studio as much as Lester would allow.

162

When he would request her assistance, she advised him about the placement of art work within the studio. Raymer also valued her critiques about the progress of work. It was Ramona Raymer who promoted Lester Raymer by sending articles to newspapers, keeping clippings of these events, and arranging for groups to tour the studio. Ramona was also the bookkeeper for the business. Raymer often told customers that he had to check with his wife about payments they could make. Later, when Morton Interiors and the Könstverk Gallery in Lindsborg became sales galleries for Raymer, Ramona Raymer continued her role in keeping track of the finances.

For a period of time Ramona Raymer took a job at the Swedish Crown Restaurant in Lindsborg. The Swedish Crown, at that time, had imports for sale in the north room and served dining guests in the south side. She brought home wooden boxes and other "goodies" from the Crown for Raymer which he would often transform into art. Most of all, because Ramona Raymer did not like to cook, she traded her work at the Crown for meals. She arranged for gallery space to be set aside at the Swedish Crown for Lester to exhibit his artwork. Lester also assisted at the Swedish Crown. He did many of their repair and remodeling tasks; even washing the dishes during special festival times.

163

WORLD'S LEADING CERAMIC CERAMIC JOURNAL

CERAMIC INDUSTRY

OCTOBER, 1949

THE RED BARN

• Lester and Ramona Raymer, both versatile artists, build a studio-home and set their sights on a Crafts-Art Center for Lindsborg, Kansas.

E. T. Martin
Lyons, Kansas

Photos by Charles Hemry

Made from two barns which were moved in, reconditioned and decorated, The Red Barn is the studio-home of Lester and Ramona Raymer of Lindsborg, Kansas. Lester Raymer, who is equally adept in every medium of art, whether it be oil, water color, graphic arts, metal work, wood-carving, jewelry making or ceramics, did much of the interior work on the building.

Emphasis On Ceramics

During the past year the Raymer's have placed emphasis on ceramics and a brief survey of the numerous pieces they have made shows their special liking for madonna figurines and roosters. Each madonna and child effectively displays full range variations in both color and ornamentation, ranging from subtle flesh tints to the vivid blues and terra cotta of the resplendent costumes. The rooster figurines, flamboyant with gleaming feathers, possess an amazing gaiety.

Use Simplified Molds

Although a potter's wheel is a recent addition to the equipment at The Red Barn, most of the figurines are cast from simplified molds, from which the intricate and ornate designs are completed. Many of the colors are derived from natural clay colorings, highlighted by clear transparent glazes. Others are stained clay, or glazes, employ the use of colored glazes.

Unique Promotion

At present the work is being sold directly from the studio, and demand has been exceeding output. Hand-blocked folders which accompany Raymer ceramics describe their origin:

"Out of the earth, clay from the hills of Kansas combine with the skill and tradition of a craft as old as man . . . plus water—air—and fire . . . comes the Red Barn Pottery made in Lindsborg, Kansas by Ramona and Lester Raymer.

"Thrown, cast, modeled, carved, inlaid, painted . . . glazed with jewel-like colors, these vases, tile, figurines and sculpture of bird, man and beast are a bequest of added beauty to the earth from which it comes."

Set Art Center As Goal

Raymer's ultimate goal is to enlarge his studios so he can handle classes in ceramics and painting. Later he hopes to import young artists and establish a Crafts-Art Center where each artist can pursue his own special talents. Raymer is a graduate of the Art Institute of Chicago, where he was honored on graduation with the Theodore Magnus Brand award for being the outstanding student of composition. He is a three time winner of the Anna Louise Raymond scholarship. He has shown his paintings, which are definitely modern in composition and color, at many important midwestern shows, and he won the Eugene Larton Gold Medal and Purchase Prize at the Philbrook Museum of Tulsa, Okla.

ENAMEL • GLASS • POTTERY

CLAY TRANSFORMED INTO POTTERY

At the end of the summer of 1947, Raymer returned to Lindsborg from Taos. He was excited about establishing the Red Barn Craft Studio. (In the late 1950s it would become the Red Barn Studio.) Raymer purchased a kiln, had a potters wheel made, and began making pottery. The kiln was kept inside the studio but the wedging table, used for removing air from clay, was kept outside as long as weather permitted. Initially Raymer knew very little about working with clay. As with any material he chose to use, he figured things out by reading, asking friends, and using "common sense." It seemed to Raymer that pottery production would be a good way to provide an income.

When Raymer began pottery production, he and Ramona worked together digging red low-fire clay from deposits south of Lindsborg. Raymer transformed the clay into roosters, Madonnas, Virgin of the Guadeloupe images, angel candleholders similar to ones he had seen in Mexico, figurine statues of Swedish and Pennsylvania Dutch men and women, and other figurines. He used thin slabs of clay to test glazes, then broke them into small pieces to use for mosaics. Clay bowls with Greek iconography, hand built ashtrays, clay tiles with embossed designs, animal sculptures, and figures of St. Francis were also a part of this clay production. Early clay works made for production sales were usually signed with three stamps; a small rooster for good luck, a red barn identifying the Red Barn Craft Studio, and his initials, LR. The clay pieces he made as one of a kind sculptures were signed "Raymer."

Raymer often created an original figurine and then made a plaster mold to use for casting multiples of the image. From this mold, he would use slip, a liquid clay, to cast multiples of the image. Raymer considered these cast figurines to be "potboilers," things sold to make a living. The roosters produced by slip casting ranged in size from approximately 6 inches to 18 inches. Many had very bright colors. Some of the figurines had a simple outline detailed with stain or underglaze. A clear glaze applied over the design allowed the red clay body to show. Ramona assisted with the glazing for the first several years. Eventually, Ramona chose not to be involved in the creative process. Instead, several artist friends helped Raymer with this work. Art students, fellow artists and friends were at the studio frequently during the 1950s assisting Raymer in creating ceramic work and mosaics.

Raymer "cranked" out ashtrays to sell as potboilers. He writes in 1948, "They are hand shaped, rather irregular in shape. The ones I have in process

165

Right: Untitled, clay Madonna and Child, from a private collection.

Below, L to R:
Clay Ashtray, Red Barn Studio.

Old jug with handpainted design by Raymer, Red Barn Studio.

Commercial dinnerware with design by Raymer, gift to Raymer Society from Gordon and Mary Reist.

now are terracotta red with the motif and band around the edge done in white glaze with black and dark gray with the motif in blue or yellow glaze. One could use most any of the colored clays for the ground with the edge and motive (decoration) done in a line of glaze. The background left unglazed." Other potboilers Raymer produced were made with commercial dinnerware. He over-painted a design on these plates with pigment or stain and then re-fired them at an extremely low temperature to set the stain. Commercially made serving trays and old crocks also became surfaces for paintings. These were signed, "hand painted by Lester Raymer."

Two major festivals in Lindsborg had a tremendous impact on sales and the promotion of the Red Barn Craft Studio. The Messiah week is a music and art festival held each year at Bethany College from Palm Sunday through Easter Sunday. The HyllningsFest festival is a community festival held bi-annually, in odd years in October (although there was a festival held in 1948). It is a celebration of the Bethany College homecoming weekend, the Swedish heritage of the settlers who founded the community, and the pioneer heritage. Raymer and his wife were involved in the festivals, both in preparation and in setting up their own sales booth during festival time.

Raymer introduced his "potboilers" at the 1948 HyllningsFest:

> "Preparation is running smoothly along toward the festival, except the pottery, it creaks and groans, only ten pieces ready for the first fire - I have got to speed things up. Mother has my costume almost complete and am I a gay thing. It will take a lot of nerve to venture forth in it the first time.

*Have decided to do the three wise men in a tile and try to sell them
for x-mas. Just another potboiler so I won't dwell on it." His next
letter states, "Ran off one of the new tiles today. Wise men came out
of the mold OK. Now to make a mold for the rooster tile. Deeply
dissatisfied with my way of life here. The hours are so long and yet I
have little to show for them."*

The Raymers painted designs on store front windows as part of their
community contribution to the HyllningsFest. Raymer wrote to Greer, "The
unveiling of the store windows is over. We all dressed up in our Svesk
costumes and paraded the streets. I was really a colorful sight. Tomorrow I
must paint a sign to put uptown directing the hordes of people to the Red
Barn." He and Ramona set up merchandise in a store front on Main Street
during festivals, or sometimes, simply a table on the sidewalk with their wares.

The Raymers sold artwork at HyllningsFest and other Lindsborg festivals for many years. The festivals were an important venue for developing of
customers for Raymer's art. Customers at the festivals included Bethany
College students and their families, individuals in town for the festival, and
people from the community. Bethany alumni who visit the studio now
comment frequently that the HyllningsFest was how they first knew about
Raymer. Customers at festivals would visit the Red Barn Craft Studio, sometimes many years later, to purchase paintings, drawings and prints.

168

After the 1948 HyllningsFest, Ramona wrote to Greer that, "We sold a lot of pottery Friday and Saturday ($155.50) and then Sunday and Monday callers bought more pottery." In 1950 after the Messiah Week Raymer writes, "Getting cleaned out of stock and have no replacements, also the prints are gone." As the festivals evolved and Raymer's business grew, he was less involved with the actual festivals and more inclined to simply open the studio during festival times. Business continued to grow through this manner for a time, but by the HyllningsFest 1969, Raymer wrote to Smith, "Sold half of what we did last year."

From November, 1947 through May of 1950, Raymer had constant trouble with his kiln and potters wheel. The insulation on the kiln needed attention. More overwhelming than the technical problems was his wish for a bigger kiln so he could make larger sculptures. Several visits to the black-smith shop were required to fix a shaft on the bearing for the potters wheel. Finally the wheel was dismantled and, "...if it doesn't perform better this time I'll use it for firewood," Raymer wrote to Greer. In 1950 Raymer got a new kiln and was finally pleased with the "yet again" rebuilt potters wheel.

Already, in 1949, Raymer saw that the clay business might be success-ful. "Our shelves are beginning to show great gaps. I'm falling behind. Is it possible that we are going to make a go of this!" He wonders, "where will this lead to?" Raymer wrote to Greer that he was "becoming artist potter of the plains." Raymer told reporters that in the 1940s and 1950s he made a living with pottery. As Raymer's reputation grew and visitors to the studio increased, changes were made in the manner in which the studio was promoted. "Ramona and I are planning to design a block print cover about the Red Barn Craft Studio. I spent an entire day cutting the block, it is tedious," Raymer wrote to Greer in 1949. Ramona's name was listed right next to Lester's name on this studio promotional card.

169

Greer's sister and brother-in-law bought roosters and watercolors in 1948. The brother-in-law expressed an interest in a big clay bull. Raymer later wrote to Greer, "I struggled a moment and finally put away my impulse to give it to him. This is what happens to me when anyone I like much admires my work as they did. If only one didn't have to make money to live."

"The British Majesty Counsel of Kansas stopped by the studio while in town for the Messiah. They had come for the Messiah - but it was The Red Barn Studio that sent them into ecstasy," Raymer wrote to Greer. Letters from 1948 through 1950 repeatedly talk about, "a constant stream of sight-seers at the studio." This constant stream of visitors began to take its toll on Raymer. By 1950 he was writing about being exhausted both physically and mentally to the point where he was neglecting pottery production. By 1957 Raymer, referring to the work it was to keep up clay production, was wonder-ing, "When will this ever stop?"

The Red Barn Craft Studio began to produce an income by the early 1950s. By 1959 Raymer wrote, "I have been lazy the first months of '59. We did so well last year. Our taxes were really something this year. Decided,

almost, that there was no use knocking one self out. We grossed nearly $7,000 last year - can you believe that? Odd thing about it is that we saved no more than wc did in carlier years when I made much less. Need the place in Taos, not only for incentives to work but could probably work out some way of spending some money that would be deductible when tax time comes along." In 1960 Raymer was, "...even worried about making too much for taxes now." In 1962 he wrote about a good sales year but laments, "Where does the money go?" The pattern continued, so that by 1975 Raymer wrote, "Last year was the best year I ever had in spite of the depression (referring to his failing health)."

George Boles recounted that the IRS, being convinced that there must be a clay quarry or a manufacturing business because of the sales, actually visited the Red Barn Craft Studio. Raymer showed them where he dug the clay and Ramona explained that her work was that of housewife. They were finally satisfied - but not until they had made a full inspection of the studio.

Sometime in the 1950s or 1960s the kiln was moved to the back garage on the north side of the studio. One day in 1970

Top: Drawing for sculpture on page 170, from a letter to Greer, 1949.

Below: Costume design from letter to Greer, Raymer Society Archives.

the kiln didn't shut off automatically. The continuous heat caused the roof of the garage to smolder. Raymer said it was an omen: that it was time to quit working with clay altogether. He sold his kiln, all his clay equipment, and ceased working with clay. Raymer told reporters, "I exhausted the medium (clay)."

Lester and Ramona at HyllningsFest, 1948. Photo from Raymer Society Archives.

WOOD, CLAY, AND METAL TRANSFORMED INTO SCULPTURE

Raymer's sculptures were produced with wood, clay and metal - although he used papier maché techniques for some of the small figures. His sculptures included images of the Madonna and Christ Child, the Virgin of Guadeloupe, St. Francis, candlesticks, carving on furniture, New Mexico type Santos, clay busts of his artist friends and brightly glazed slip-cast roosters averaging 12 to 18 inches in height. He also worked with concrete, creating plaster molds or sand-casting smaller forms. Raymer created concrete sculptures for the studio including an eagle, small statues and planters for the courtyard, and two lion columns for the fireplace in the south studio. Dale Hoag went to the Nelson-Atkins Museum of Art in Kansas City, Missouri, to obtain photographs of the lion columns on display to serve as reference material for Raymer.

As the pottery business grew, Raymer turned his focus away from the "potboilers" toward single, one of a kind clay sculptures. The artistic satisfaction Raymer found in working with clay came through sculptures he created. "Finishing another Europa and bull today and starting another St. Francis tomorrow. Have a commission to do Jonah and the Whale." Raymer describes a St. Francis he is creating, "I am doing him in a red clay. If satisfying in color and surface texture will leave him in the bisque." Letters to Greer continued to document the clay sculptures Raymer was making. "Did I tell you I glazed the boar? I worked out an overall linear design of glaze stripes and spots as the sketch, crude - used the light blue calamine. Then I stained it dark gray. Is quite effective. I'm full of ideas for other things using the same technique."

In the spring of 1949 Raymer wrote, "I was up quite late last night and up early this morning to finish another sculpture. St. Francis again. The largest piece that I have fired. It is done in red clay." He also exclaims that he

Original cover designs for program booklets, HyllningsFest 1985 and 1971.

Below: Ramona setting up window display for HyllningFest, Raymer Society Archives.

174

has, "at last found a glaze," for the clay sculptures. A ceramic David and Eve are the focus of Raymer's November 1949 letter. "Finished Eve in clay, she stands as high as the kiln will allow her to stand. She was fun to do although I'm not too happy with her. She is not long and lean enough and too heavy hipped." In the 1950s Raymer and George Boles bought a large odd shaped metal container which they then cast a concrete form around to create a water pond. Raymer then made a red clay St. Francis sculpture, attached it to the south wall of the front garage, and surrounded it in bricks. The cement/metal pond was placed beneath this sculpture.

In 1950 Raymer began to use brazing and welding techniques to create sculptures from wire and metal, and often, from recycled objects. These metal sculptures were based on the rooster, circus jugglers and acrobats. One wall hanging is a metal rooster Raymer made by tearing apart a metal Christmas tree using the limbs to create the rooster's feathers. It is hard to place actual dates for some of these wire and metal sculptures, but research indicates that most of them were made from 1950 to 1966. The sculptures varied in size from only six inches to more than eighteen inches tall.

Religious imagery was a continuing theme in Raymer's sculptures as well as in his other artwork. "I grew bored with wood carving and set them aside and took up a new medium. Out of sheets of lead I pounded out a crucifix. The figure is about 20" high mounted on a polished walnut cross. It was a lot of fun and a rest from carving." In the spring of 1950, he was working on ideas for a possible commission for a church in Concordia, Kansas, and "Madonna and Child sculptures." Greer wrote to Raymer, "The new Madonna

Left: Processional cross for St. Andrews Episcopal Church, Emporia, Kansas.

Right: Baptismal Font, Gloria Dei Lutheran Church, Houston, Texas.

Below: Clay sculpture of Milford Greer, gift to Raymer Society from Peter and Irene Kennedy.

175

- I do not know what to say about a thing so fine. The strength, the majesty, and the beautiful surface are greatly impressive."

A mosaic altar piece was created for the Catholic Church in Russell, Kansas, in the spring of 1955. Raymer tells Greer that, "it looks so simple after completion. It belies the hours and hours of tedious labor of setting the bits of tile. The crucifix completed a year ago will not be hung till these panels are done." In the summer of 1960, Raymer wrote, "been up since five a.m. finishing up a metal sculpture of the Madonna and Child for the Michigan show." He was referring to the National Religious Art exhibition where his "Madonna and Child" won first place. In addition to commission work, Raymer created small metal crosses which were sold to individuals. These crosses play a major role in the owners' lives. In 1950, Jane Dronberger, Hutchinson, Kansas, for example, requested that her bride's gift from the groom be a Raymer cross, rather than the traditional string of pearls.

Some of the sculptures and liturgical commissions included mosaic work. The materials utilized in the mosaics were from items Raymer got at auctions, clay slabs he used for glaze testing, glass pieces, and bathroom tiles. Students from Bethany and artist friends that visited the studio became involved with his mosaic work. In 1962, Raymer was creating mosaic work for the home in Taos, for wall pieces, and some for sale. That year he sent a mosaic to the National Religious Art exhibition in Michigan. Sometimes Raymer used mosaic techniques to obtain the effect of stained glass by sandwiching colored glass pieces between a pieces clear glass. Much of the basic material for this process was transformed from old 7-Up bottles, melted down and then broken.

176

Raymer used clay to model busts of several of his artist friends. Some of these were then cast in bronze. Since Raymer did not have the facilities for casting he had to depend on other artists for this process. Thus he did not continue to do much with bronze casting.

To keep his hands busy while watching television, Raymer transformed tin can lids into tin stars in a variety of designs. Tin snips were used to cut the shapes and needle nose pliers were used to do the twisting design work. These stars were sold at festivals and at the studio, but more often, they were shared as gifts for friends and family at Christmas time. Occasionally, Raymer would use larger portions of industrial size cans to develop tin crosses.

TRANSFORMING TO CREATE JEWELRY

In addition to the clay figurines, tiles, bowls and other functional clay work, Raymer transformed clay into jewelry to sell at festivals. It was an inexpensive item he had at the studio for those people who might not otherwise have been able to afford a purchase. This clay was shaped into small faces or sun images which Raymer referred to as "uglies." He made clay beads of assorted shapes to place on a leather string with the "ugly." Designs were carved into the beads. The uglies and the beads were usually not glazed, just wiped with a color stain to allow the red clay body to be the primary focus. Raymer created a mold and then pressed clay into the mold to form the uglies. Occasionally, he carved designs on damp peach pits and then, when dry, used them as the mold for his clay designs.

In addition to these uglies, Raymer would make small clay figures, similar to ancient pottery figures from Mexico, as jewelry pieces. He also made clay stars for jewelry and as a mold for shaping light weight metal into stars, various

Top: Assortment of tin stars.

Below: One of the "uglies."
Raymer Society Archives.

sculptures, or toys. Small coin-shaped clay pieces were impressed with designs and stained. These became items anyone could afford. Sometimes Raymer simply gave them to visitors.

Using the lost wax casting technique, Raymer made several rings for himself. He created metal necklaces with fine jewel insets and carved ivory for pins and inserts in rings. Many antique pieces of jewelry were transformed into new jewelry. Raymer often sought out Malcolm Esping's insight when he created jewelry. This transformation from old jewelry into new was similar to his toy creations. Ramona had a passion for antique jewelry, but since they could not afford to collect jewelry, Raymer created pieces of jewelry for her.

TRANSFORMATION OF FURNITURE

Both in his Oklahoma studio and in the Red Barn Studio, the furniture Raymer transformed was important to the attitude of the studio itself and usually was not for sale. Very few pieces of furniture which entered his studios remained "as is." He altered the doors and added metal work and hinges of his own creation. Raymer transformed the base plate of the old locks and created elaborate top layers of metal with serpents, sun images, turtle, and fish. To create etched designs in metal, Raymer secured a piece of paper to the surface, drew the design in pencil, and then used tools such as dental tools to scratch in the design.

178

Painted cabinet and carved candlesticks from central room, Red Barn Studio.

Some of the furniture was transformed of necessity when the Raymers married. Other pieces were transformed in anticipation of moving to Taos. Still other pieces were moved from his studio in Oklahoma. The Raymers held annual garage sales for a period of years. Some lucky individuals bought furniture, realizing only after they got home that it was a piece of furniture transformed in some way by Raymer.

Raymer collected old furniture at sales, through trading, and from friends. He saw furniture as surfaces for creative transformation—sometimes, even as surfaces for his painting. On the front and two side panels of a wardrobe, Raymer painted a surreal painting in the style of DeChirico. He altered the door panels of most pieces of furniture. Sometimes this would mean simply adding moldings of different sizes to trim out the doors. Some furniture was painted and elaborate carvings Raymer created were added to the door panels. Raymer in his June 1969 letter to Greer writes, "finished more or less the new cupboard. I call it the Apostles Cupboard. It is made from the old Dutch door that I replaced last fall. Has the twelve panels on the front on each of which I have carved one of the apostles. The wrought iron fittings were fun to do and it is rather a handsome piece." Raymer also describes a "nice little chest that I converted from Swedish to Spanish. It

makes a handsome piece and will fit well in the adobe (referring to the Taos home)." Since this letter was not mailed when intended, Raymer added an additional letter which states, "finished the apostle cabinet and moved it to the back room at the foot of the stairs where the white pie cabinet used to be. The new Spanish chest is replacing the round coffee table. We have enough furniture to furnish another house, here and in Taos."

Raymer transformed the surface of a wooden divider screen into a surface for a painting. This painted screen is the only one of its kind as far as anyone knows. One time, someone gave Raymer a broken rocking horse. He fixed it, cleaned it, and then repainted it. The horse sat upstairs on the landing in the north studio area until one day a woman, who was obviously pregnant, visited the studio. She admired the horse. As she was getting ready to leave, Raymer told her the horse wasn't really for sale but she looked like she needed it for the child. The rocking horse remains a treasure for the grown child.

In the central area of the Red Barn Studio is a desk which Raymer made for Ramona. One day she showed him a picture of a really beautiful desk in a magazine and talked about how nice it would be to have one like it. Raymer obtained a large wooden box and proceeded to make Ramona the beautiful desk. He made metalwork latches with a horse head design, a serpent clasp, and forged scallop sea shells to surround the edge of the desk. Raymer also pounded and shaped metal into a sun for the front decoration. An existing furniture base was used to hold the box. Carved lion heads attached to the glide board serve as a rest for the lid when open. The open lid reveals inner drawers which Raymer has transformed from scraps of wood he faced with samples of embossed leather. The edges of the drawers are scrap trim board painted red. The lions' head pulls are ones Raymer cast from a commercially made model. The overall visual effect is a beautiful desk. The aesthetics of the total image was of prime concern to Raymer, not necessarily the function. Most of the drawers have little or no interior structure. The desk remained in the Red Barn Studio, apparently never moved to the house for Ramona to use.

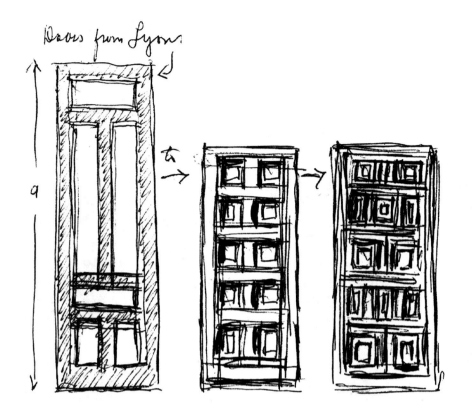

From a letter written by Raymer discussing found doors and their possible uses in the Lindsborg and Taos studios.

Today, seeing the furniture in place in the Red Barn Studio, one realizes the significance of the furniture to the total aesthetic of the studio. Each cabinet served as a storage unit for Raymer magazines, art supplies, tools, and the "stuff" he collected. In some cabinets, he stored materials destined to be parts for the next toy project. His record player and record collection were in one cabinet. And, in the green cabinet, there was a small television, hidden from the public. The transformed furniture sits in the same rooms with antique day beds, 1950s chairs, ancient oriental cabinets, and assorted straight chairs.

FABRIC SAMPLES, THREADS, BROKEN JEWELRY TRANSFORMED INTO BANNERS

The stitchery skills Raymer learned from his mother were transformed into skills for creating banners in the 1960s. Ramona says Lester took up stitchery to help him stay awake while watching television. Raymer said he viewed the banners as a hobby and as items for the adornment of the walls of the studio, not created to sell.

As with other work, Raymer set up a work area with his thread, fabric, jewels, and yarn by the television in the Raymer's home. The sewing machine was placed on a small table next to him. Thus, he was able to watch TV and keep his hands busy creating. Raymer had an incredible eye for envisioning how fabric sample pieces would work together. Each banner incorporates symbols Raymer used in his other art forms; the sun, the fish, the moon, the Madonna and Child, and others.

181

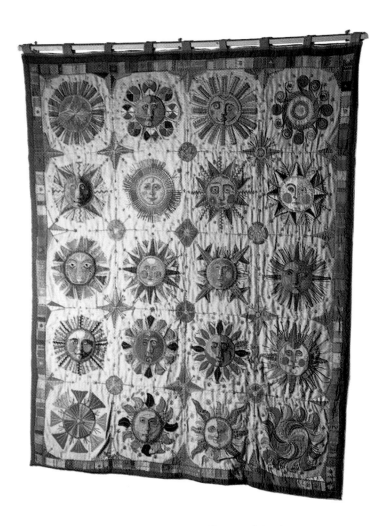

Some of the banners are completely machine stitched. The shadowing created with zig-zag stitches and multiple colored threads portrays an in-depth understanding of drawing. The moon/sun banner with a blue felt back-ground includes samples of loose weave curtain fabric placed to form the moon/sun face and rays. Zig-zag stitchery was used as a drawing tool to model the face of the moon/sun, to connect the pieces, and to outline. The result is an image of the sun and moon merging.

Raymer created a simple sun banner using a red cloth background. This banner was placed in the yard on a long pole to announce to the public that the studio was open. The banner was used in the 1970s and 1980s for Lindsborg Open House events–designated times when artists and galleries were open to the public. To carry on Raymer's tradition, the Raymer Society replicated the banner as a sign in 1997, using wood rather than cloth to enhance durability and visibility.

The large Sun Quilt banner hanging in the central part of the studio was done over a two year period of time, from 1964 to 1965. Each section was created as a separate block and then stitched together as a quilt. A Lindsborg resident visited the studio in 1996. She told how some of the women in the community were upset when they discovered Raymer was

182

doing stitchery as part of his artwork. They sent her to tell him that stitchery was a woman's work. "Later, when we saw how skilled he was and the beauty he created, well, we started bringing him only our finest threads, many of which became a part of the large sun banner." The complexity of the stitchery combined with the color and textural selection of threads create a dynamic image.

The Madonna and Child banners integrate stitchery with beads, jewels, and trims, to create images reflecting elements of Mexican, Byzantine and Russian art. The underlying imagery in these Madonna and Child banners is from the Catholic religion. The richness of the background fabric, the jewels, and the expressions elevate the Madonna and Child beyond the depiction of a mother and her child to the realm of the holy.

Boxes and Trunks Transformed

Shipping boxes, wooden household boxes, immigrant trunks, and an assortment of other trunks found their way to the Red Barn Studio. Some were purchased by the Raymers at garage sales and auctions. Some were discards that individuals gave to Raymer. Others were from retail businesses who received merchandise in boxes. When Raymer began buying immigrant

Facing page: Sun Quilt, hand stitched banner, 1964-65.

This page, left to right: Red "The Studio is Open" banner, nd.

Two Madonna and Child banners, combination of machine and hand stitchery, nd.

All items in Red Barn Studio.

183

*Hinge and furniture ideas—
sketches from letters
written by Raymer.*

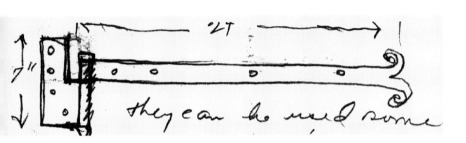

trunks at Lindsborg area auctions, they sold for very little money. Then, as individuals noted Raymer always bought these trunks, people began to think the trunks must be valuable, and so the bidding wars began. At this point Raymer lost interest in the trunks. He also lost interest in the trunks because, after he transformed a trunk into a work of art, families would come to the studio to claim that the trunk should have never been sold: that it belonged in the family.

Large boxes and trunks served as significant surfaces for Raymer's artwork. He viewed the boxes and trunks as surfaces to display his creative vision, almost as if the surfaces were canvas. Some boxes appear to be studies for furniture or other creations. Some have elaborate metal work, carvings, or designs added to the surface.

Smaller boxes were transformed into art using a variety of surface treatments. Some boxes were painted using traditional folk painting techniques, created specifically as "pot boilers" to sell at festivals. Other boxes were made for use in the studio. Wallpaper samples, foil paper, or marbled paper were used to line the interiors of boxes Raymer created for sale or as gifts for Ramona. Boxes created for use in the studio usually had unfinished interiors.

One small box is decoupaged with cut out images of the human figure and a fish on top of a surface of road maps. This decoupage box appears to be a document or comment on the trip Ramona, Lan Nelson and Raymer made to Europe in 1970. Another is painted with patterns similar to the harlequin costumes in Raymer's paintings. The pattern and colors of this particular box are identical to the background on one of the icons Raymer

184

Examples of Raymer's metal work, created for doors and boxes, Raymer Society Archives.

painted. Raymer carved the twelve disciples and a sun face into the surfaces of one box. Traditional Swedish chip carving techniques were utilized on some box surfaces. At Christmas Raymer created jewelry boxes for Ramona as gifts. One such gift was a set of nested boxes painted with a simplistic folk painting motif.

Raymer used blacksmithing techniques to create elaborate metal work on locks and handles for boxes and trunks. Serpents and turtles are the most common images used in the lock sections of the boxes. Sometimes an old lock on the box was incorporated into the design. Some of the handles are attached using metal suns or sea shells Raymer designed. He also created the metal hinges and strapping elements wrapped around the boxes. An interesting observation can be made in the patterns of Raymer's metal work hinges. They appear very much like traditional cutout paper patterns used by the native Indian communities in Mexico as ceremonial decorations.

In the 1950s Raymer experimented with sheet copper into which he embossed or hammered designs. The sheet was then used to wrap objects, including boxes, to serve as the decorative surface. Some of these copper wrapped boxes became vessels for storing a chalice or other such items created as gifts for special friends.

Boxes and trunks are in every part of the studio. One visitor to the studio expressed that the boxes look like treasures of the past ready to hold treasures of the future. Another person concluded that Raymer had turned these boxes and trunks into Medieval treasures. When the studio restoration began, each of Raymer's boxes was emptied and cleaned.

A

B

C

D

E

F

G

H

I

J

Apparently Raymer created these boxes as practical containers for his own "stuff" and art supplies. Each box contained a variety of materials; assorted junk, thread, clay pieces, sketches, and much more. Larger boxes and trunks stored guns and parts for guns, fabric, quilts, magazines, and paper samples.

TRANSFORMING FOR LIGHT

Candleholders were made by Raymer in his studio in Oklahoma as a necessity and in Lindsborg as images crafted to enhance studio aesthetics. One chandelier was transformed by Raymer from the wood rim of a wagon wheel and parts of farm tools. Several hanging metal chandeliers were made using iron and scrap pieces from various tools, lamps, old cook stove handles, and formed sheet metal. Raymer used spindles and table legs as tall candlesticks incorporating his carved designs of saints or apostles. The candle holders sitting on the bay window ledge in the north side of the studio are pitchforks, transformed into candle holders. The liturgical commissions Raymer received often included candlesticks. Raymer relied on Malcolm Esping to assist him in fulfilling some of these commissions. Esping did most of the work

Boxes and techniques:

A. Painted surface.
B. Swedish Folk Painting.
C. Painted, with metal work.
D. Carved, with metal work
E. Decoupaged with materials related to European trip.
F. Metal studded surface treatment.
G. Chip carving.
H. Nested boxes with folk painting.
I. Chip carving and metal work.
J. "Needle Box" with copper overlay.
K. Carving of Apostles, with metal work.

Red Barn Studio and Raymer Society Collection.

K

on candlesticks designed by Raymer for the Topeka and Emporia, Kansas church commissions.

One year Ramona's Christmas gift from Raymer was a set of candleholders modeled after Czechoslovakian wedding candlesticks. After their trip to Europe, Raymer created short metal candlesticks for their dining table like those he had seen in Spain.

Masks Transformed from Scraps

Raymer created masks following many traditional forms. His work in Oklahoma was primarily papier maché clown masks. In Kansas, Raymer seems to have been influenced by traditional mask forms from diverse cultures. He used papier maché techniques to create the forms on some masks while others were carved and shaped from wood.

Ramona brought home masks when she traveled. These served as models for transforming materials into masks of Raymer's own design. When he was asked about the history of the masks; which ones he made, and which ones were "real," Raymer replied, "It doesn't matter."

THE LEGACY

What mattered most for Lester Raymer was his ability to visually describe his artistic perceptions, transforming ordinary materials into objects of aesthetic expression.

Raymer wrote a short journal his last few years of life. His thoughts lead one to consider how his work transforms a viewer's perceptions and visions of the world. Two of the entries are especially poignant as a summary of Raymer's life and his artwork.

"The test of a great work of Art is its immediate impact on the viewer. One should see it and react. An overall sense of the work should arouse you, move you, give you an emotional and aesthetic boost."

"Genius is an abstraction which comes to life when its possessor dies. Then his creations start to live, assuming that they have any life at all, for they occupy the place where he stood when he looked at the world, and they offer to those who know how to see it, a vision of what he saw, what he stood for, and what he created for others to look at."

Left to right:
Untitled, pair of candelabras, metal work. Created in Lester's Alma Studio, Oklahoma, nd.

Untitled, candelabra, metal work, nd.

Candle stand with carving of Apostles, wood, nd.

Below: Untitled, carved horse candleholder, wood, nd.

All works in Red Barn Studio.

Interior of Red Barn Studio,
1998 photo by Jim Richardson.

Acknowledgments

This book would not be possible without the generous sharing of thoughts and memories by individuals which were interviewed. Although many individuals shared and many individuals assisted with preparations for the book, the contributing writers want to especially thank:

Rita Sharpe, John Bergers, Dale Hoag, Rick and Marilyn Nelson, John and Jan Raymer, Edna Raymer, Mr. and Mrs. Jack King, Father Frank Coady, Gretchen Esping Swanson, the late Dr. Greta Swenson, Althea and Royer Barclay, Jud Barclay, Birgit Hegewald and Margaret Stromquist for their interviews, research time, and editing.

Peter and Irene Kennedy, in addition to a personal interview, shared letters from Lester to Milford Greer and from Milford Greer to Lester Raymer. Larry Smith shared many conversations through phone calls and also shared letters from Lester to himself as well as other archival material.

Elane O'Rourke, Rosann Cedarholm, the late Virginia Ericson, Gail and Earland Olson, and Ila and Marvin Johnson assisted in sorting files to arrange the Raymer Society Archives. Julie Taylor, an art major at Bethany College, spent a semester as an intern helping to organize the Raymer archives. Lauren Kahler assisted in arranging photographs. Jean Kozubowski is the volunteer Photo Archivist for the Raymer Society.

Thank you to those individuals who contributed to the financial support for research related to this book, especially Bill and Carol Gusenius and Frank Grippy.

Friends and family of each of the writers, thank you for understanding the time it takes to research and write.

Assemblage, nd, Red Barn Studio.

The Authors

Bruce R. Kahler is Associate Professor of History at Bethany College, Lindsborg, Kansas, where he teaches courses in American History and European Art History. Kahler has written numerous brief articles, book reviews for professional journals, historical encyclopedia entries, and op-ed pieces for the *Salina Journal*. He received his BA in history from Kutztown (PA) State College, his MA and Ph.D. in history at Purdue University. His dissertation topic was "Art and Life: The Arts and Crafts Movement in Chicago, 1897-1910." Kahler lives in Lindsborg, Kansas, with his wife, Caroline, and children, Lauren and Andrew. Caroline is head of the Art Department at Bethany College and Lauren is a Raymer Society docent.

Dr. Kahler wishes to thank Carla Scott for her invaluable research assistance and unfailing encouragement. He dedicates the essay to his wife, Caroline, and their children, Lauren and Andrew.

Diane Thomas Lincoln is an artist and educator. Lincoln is Certificate Program Director of Decorative and Ornamental Painting and Design at the School of Art and Design, Wichita State University. She has taught various classes and workshops on visual art and theology for numerous institutions throughout the United States and abroad. Diane's artwork has been published on the covers of numerous national and international magazines and journals. She maintains an active exhibition and lecture schedule among the commissions which she and her husband, Gary R. Lincoln, receive for sacred and secular art.

Don Weddle is an artist and retired arts educator. As an educator in the Wichita Public Schools for over 30 years, Weddle has influenced many students to achieve national status in their chosen art. Weddle's studio is at Prairiewood Gallery in Lindsborg, Kansas. He and his wife, Johnell, live in Wichita, Kansas, while spending part of each week in Lindsborg. A major retrospective of his work was held at the Birger Sandzén Memorial Art Gallery in 1997. In 1988, Weddle published an article for *Southwest Art* on Lester Raymer.

Lan Nelson is a 1972 graduate of Wichita State University with a BA in English and an Elementary Teaching Certificate from Bethany College, Lindsborg, Kansas. He presently lives in Lindsborg where he is Director of Activities for Bethany Home, an intermediate care facility. He has an interest in collecting old toys, restoration of his home, traveling and making tin Christmas ornaments, a craft he learned from Lester Raymer in 1979.

Carla Scott is an artist and arts administrator. She is the full time director of the Raymer Society. Carla and her husband, Steve Scott, have their artwork for show and sale at their home studio, Studio Two. Scott has her Ph.D. in Education and Administration from The Ohio State University with a second masters in Studio Arts and Arts Administration from University of South Florida. Scott has published numerous curriculum guides, statewide handbooks for educators, and in-service teacher education materials. She has curated regional and national art exhibitions. Her own artwork has been exhibited in group shows, one and two person shows, and at outdoor art fairs.

LESTER RAYMER AND HIS ART WORLD, BY BRUCE R. KAHLER

ABBREVIATIONS:

LN-R   Lindsborg News-Record
LR   Lester Raymer
LS   Larence (Larry) Smith
LSPP   Larence Smith Private Papers
MG   Milford Greer
MGP   Milford Greer Papers, Mennonite Library and Archives, North Newton, Kansas
RR   Ramona Raymer
RSA   Raymer Society Archives, Lindsborg, Kansas

FOOTNOTES

1   Peggy Greene, "Peggy of the Flint Hills," *Topeka Daily Capital,* 1 March 1956.
2   Ibid.
3   Ibid.
4   Peggy Greene to LR and RR, December 1955, RSA.
5   Peggy Greene to LR, c. February 1955, RSA.
6   My understanding of an art world is drawn largely from Howard S. Becker, *Art Worlds* (Berkeley: University of California Press, 1982).
7   See, for example, "Lindsborg's artist genius...Raymer talents honored," *LN-R,* 8 November 1984, and comments by Carl Peterson in Alan Stolfus, "Variety characterizes Lindsborg artist," *Salina Journal,* 22 August 1988; Don Weddle in Jan Biles, "Student tries to explain Lindsborg artist," *Hutchinson News,* 27 August 1988; and Diane Thomas Lincoln in Susan L. Rife, "Gifted, eclectic artist Raymer 'was a rare bird,' " *Wichita Eagle,* 4 June 1991.
8   Lester Raymer [obituary], *LN-R,* 6 June 1991.
9   Ibid. The obituary is correct in stating that Raymer was the third of four Raymer children. The first child, a daughter, died in infancy.
10 Jan Biles, "Artist who traveled the world lives out dream in Lindsborg," *Hutchinson News,* 27 August 1988.
11 John Raymer, interview by Carla Scott, tape recording, 4-5 October 1997, RSA
12 *Aurora (CO) High School Yearbook* (1926), 17, 25.
13 *Aurora (CO) High School Yearbook* (1927), 31, 32.
14 Peggy Greene, "Artist Achieves True Individuality," *Topeka Daily Capital*, 16 January 1955.
15 "Exceptionally Good Art Exhibit," *LN-R,* 29 March 1945. The *News-Record* also reported that Raymer had received the Fredrick Magnus Brand Memorial Award while at the School of the Art Institute. Raymer's transcript records the Brand Memorial Award but does not confirm that he received the Anna Louise Raymond Scholarship. The School of the Art Institute of Chicago, transcript of Lester W. Raymer (copy), 7 June 1946, RSA.
16 Don Weddle, "Lester Raymer," *Southwest Art,* August 1988, 64-65.
17 Charlotte Moser, " 'In the Highest Efficiency': Art Training at the School of the Art Institute of Chicago," in *The Old Guard and the Avant-Garde: Modernism in Chicago, 1910-1940,* ed. Sue Ann Prince (Chicago: The University of Chicago Press, 1990), 193.
18 Ibid., 202-204.
19 Weddle, "Lester Raymer," 65.
20 Moser, " 'In the Highest Efficiency,' " 206.
21 LR to MG, 2 November 1948, RSA.
22 Roger J. Mesley, *Boris Anisfeld "Fantast-Mystic": Twelve Russian Paintings from the Collection of Joey and Toby Tanenbaum* (Art Gallery of Ontario, 1989), 11-12.
23 John Raymer, interview by Carla Scott, tape recording, 4-5 October 1997, RSA.
24 Ibid.
25 The School of the Art Institute of Chicago, transcript of Lester W. Raymer (copy), 7 June 1946; Northwestern (OK) State College, transcript of Lester W. Raymer (copy), 10 April 1946, both in RSA.
26 Ginny Brandenburg to LR, 26 July 1985, RSA.
27 Weddle, "Lester Raymer," 66.
28 "The Story of Munson Mistletoe Turkeys," pamphlet, RSA.
29 Raymond Jonson to LR, 16 May 1947, RSA.
30 Philbrook Art Center, Tulsa, OK, note, 6 May 1944, RSA.
31 Emory Lindquist, *Birger Sandzén: An Illustrated Biography* (Lawrence, KS: University Press of Kansas, 1993), 79, 89.
32 Birger Sandzén to LR, 12 April 1942, RSA; Lindquist, *Birger Sandzén,* 29.
33 "Wins Prize on Oil Painting," *LN-R,* 25 May 1944.
34 Ibid.
35 "Exceptionally Good Art Exhibit."

36 The School of the Art Institute of Chicago, transcript of Ramona E. Weddle (copy), 20 September 1933, RSA.
37 Sharon Montague, "Mankato couple hopes people roam to Brunswick," *Salina Journal*, 29 April 1990.
38 Bethany College, transcript of Ramona E. Weddle (copy), 23 April 1935, RSA.
39 Ramona E. Raymer [obituary], *LN-R*, 16 July 1992.
40 "Local Artists Choose Swedish Peasant House Model of Home," *LN-R*, 10 October 1946.
41 Ibid.
42 "Art in a Red Barn," *to the Stars,* August 1950, np.
43 "Local Artists Choose."
44 Bob Nelson, "Salina Slants: Feet Itch?," *Salina Journal*, 29 March 1951.
45 "Art in a Red Barn."
46 "Local Artists Choose."
47 Bette Roth to LR, 30 November 1948; Mrs. Byron Walters to RR, 7 March 1949; Deborah Sharp to LR, 25 April 1949; Mrs. R.F. Mallory to LR, 15 September 1949; Frank Pedroja, Jr. to LR, 27 October 1949, all in RSA.
48 Handwritten note, RSA.
49 LR to MG, 30 April 1949, RSA.
50 LR to MG, 21 October 1949 and 6 April 1950, both in RSA.
51 LR to MG, 30 April 1949, RSA.
52 LR to MG, 25 April 1950, RSA.
53 LR to MG, 21 October 1949, RSA.
54 LR to MG, 6 April 1950, RSA.
55 Vicky, "'Foreign' Metalcraft Worker Joins Ranks of Lindsborg Artists," *McPherson Daily Republican,* 17 April 1946.
56 LR to MG, 17 October 1949, RSA.
57 The Lindsborg Artists' Guild, "The Arts in Lindsborg," pamphlet, RSA.
58 LR to MG, 6 November 1949, RSA.
59 LR to MG, 17 October 1949, RSA.
60 Lindsborg Artists' Guild, "The Arts in Lindsborg."
61 Ibid.; Mrs. J.R. Poland, "Art Tour of Lindsborg," *Herrington Advertiser-Times,* 4 May 1950.
62 Lindsborg Artists' Guild, "The Arts in Lindsborg."
63 Lindsborg Artists' Guild, "Art in Lindsborg," pamphlet, RSA.
64 Lindquist, *Birger Sandzén.*
65 Ibid., 111-114.
66 M.S.G. [Margaret Sandzén Greenough], "Art Gallery Notes," *LN-R*, 1 January 1958.
67 M.S.G. [Margaret Sandzén Greenough], "Art Gallery Notes," *LN-R*, 6 February 1958, 27 March 1958.
68 M.S.G. [Margaret Sandzén Greenough], "Art Gallery Notes," *LN-R*, 16 November, 1961.
69 "Raymer's retrospective exhibition begins at Sandzén," *LN-R*, 28 July 1988.
70 Lindquist, *Birger Sandzén,* 53.
71 Margaret Greenough to LR, 27 February 1958, RSA.
72 M.S.G. [Margaret Sandzén Greenough], "Art Gallery Notes," *LN-R*, 1 January 1958.
73 M.S.G. [Margaret Sandzén Greenough], "Art Gallery Notes," *LN-R*, 23 January 1958.
74 Margaret Greenough to LR, 18 June, 20 June, 24 June, 1949, RSA.
75 Margaret Greenough to LR, 17 June 1958, RSA.
76 Bob Kaiser, "Art is Preferred to Money," *Wichita Beacon,* 6 March 1957.
77 Bob Sanford, "Art Museum on the Plains Adds to Lindsborg's Lure," *Kansas City Star,* 22 June 1958.
78 Judy Farrell, "Small world of art with a Swedish touch," *Midway: the Magazine of the Topeka Capital-Journal,* 12 February 1967, 11.
79 Kay Berenson, "Kansas Art Colony," *Salina Journal Sunflower,* 8 August 1982, 10.
80 Ibid.; Joanna K. Wiebe, "Lindsborg Nourishes Kansas' Only Claim to an Art Colony," *Wichita Eagle and Beacon,* 22 October 1972.
81 Rosella Ögg, *Kansas Artists of the Present,* (Manhattan, KS: Extension Service, Kansas State University, October 1966), 6.
82 Wiebe, "Lindsborg Nourishes."
83 Quoted in ibid.
84 Berenson, "Kansas Art Colony," 10.
85 "Dr. Birger Sandzén Resigns Position," *McPherson Sentinel,* 2 May 1946.
86 My perspective on Sandzén is more fully articulated in Bruce R. Kahler, "Lindsborg and the Legacy of Birger Sandzén," *Sweden and America,* Spring 1993, 7-10. The standard work is Lindquist, *Birger Sandzén.*
87 Bethany College, contract with Lester Raymer, 29 April 1946, RSA.
88 *Bethany Messenger,* 5 November 1946.
89 *Bethany Messenger,* 17 December 1946.
90 *Bethany Messenger,* 18 March 1947.
91 *Bethany Messenger,* 19 November 1946.
92 *Bethany Messenger,,* 29 April 1947.
93 Emory Lindquist to LR, 17 April 1947, RSA.
94 LR to Emory Lindquist, 19 April 1947, RSA.
95 Lloyd H. Cowan to LR, 19 March 1947, RSA.
96 LR to Emory Lindquist, 19 April 1947, RSA.
97 LR to Emory Lindquist, 19 April 1947, RSA.

Four illustrations of Swedish Christmas traditions, by Raymer, ca 1950.

Reproduced as cards by the Raymer Society, 1997.

98   Raymond Jonson to LR, 16 May 1947, RSA.
99   Susan S. Weininger, "Modernism and Chicago Art: 1910-1940," in *The Old Guard and the Avant-Garde: Modernism in Chicago, 1910-1940,* ed. Sue Ann Prince (Chicago: The University of Chicago Press, 1990), 62-63.
100 Lindquist, *Birger Sandzén,* 58.
101 E.W. Pollock to LR, 10 December 1937, RSA.
102 Raymond Jonson to LR, 16 May 1947, RSA.
103 LR to RR, 16 June 1947, RSA.
104 LR to RR, 20 June 1947, RSA. The Field School, however, has no transcript to confirm Raymer's registration there.
105 "Plan Two Man Art Exhibit Here Soon," *LN-R,* 14 August 1947.
106 LR to RR, 21 July 1947, RSA.
107 LR to RR, 11 July 1947, RSA.
108 LR to RR, 20 June 1947, RSA.
109 LR to RR, 27 June 1947, RSA.
110 LR to RR, 28 July 1947, RSA.
111 "Plan Two Man."
112 LR to RR, 16 June 1947, RSA.
113 LR to RR, 27 June 1947, RSA.
114 LR to RR, 1 July 1947, RSA.
115 LR to RR, (?) July 1947, RSA.
116 LR to RR, 16 July 1947, RSA.
117 LR to RR, 20 June 1947, RSA.
118 "Plan Two Man."
119 LR to RR, 16 June 1947, RSA.
120 LR to RR, 27 June 1947, RSA.
121 LR to RR, 1 July 1947, RSA.
122 Ibid.
123 LR to RR, 16 July 1947, RSA.
124 LR to RR, 8 July 1947, RSA.
125 LR to RR, 1 July 1947, RSA.
126 LR to RR, 16 June 1947, RSA.
127 LR to MG, 26 January 1949, RSA.
128 Ibid.; LR to MG, 11 January 1950, RSA
129 LR to Reverend Malm, c. April 1953, RSA.
130 Emory Lindquist to LR, 17 July 1953, RSA.
131 "Raymer Ceramic Exhibit At College," *LN-R,* 25 March 1954; "Lindsborg Artists Included In Midwest Exhibit Next Week," *LN-R,* 8 April 1954; Lloyd Spear to LR, 14 December 1954, RSA.
132 "Art Students at Bethany College to Mexico City," *LN-R,* 28 December 1958; "Bethany Art Students to Mexico During Vacation," *LN-R,* 25 January 1960.
133 "Hostility Ceases at Lindsborg Over Bethany College Future," *Wichita Eagle,* 26 February 1967.
134 "Two Unusual Exhibits Open at WU Galleries," *Wichita Eagle,* 15 October 1960.
135 Quoted in Stolfus, "Variety characterizes." For similar comments see also John P. Simoni, "Kansans' Oils Emphasize Life," *Wichita Eagle and Beacon Magazine,* 19 April, 1966; and Larry Griffis quoted in Rife, "Gifted, eclectic artist."
136 Barbara Phillips, "For the Lester Raymers of Lindsborg Toys Are A Christmas Tradition," *Salina Journal Sunflower,* 13 December 1981, 12; Margaret Allen, "Pure Lester: He wants his art to speak for itself," *Wichita Eagle Beacon,* 4 September 1988.
137 Clarke Thomas, "Ceramics Or Silver, It's All Art to Him," *Hutchinson News-Herald,* 10 April 1949. This important article also appeared as "World of Art Is His Oyster," *Salina Journal,* 14 April 1949.
138 Raymer's comments in LR to MG, 22 September 1949, and later in LR to MG, 14 November 1949, RSA, suggest that he did not think his work in ceramics was as creative as his painting.
139 "Plan Two Man."
140 "New Enterprise by Local Artists," *LN-R,* 22 April 1948.
141 "Two Men Plan Art Show At Lindsborg Sunday," *McPherson Republican,* 9 September 1948.
142 *Hutchinson News-Herald,* 12 September 1948.
143 Dudley Crafts Watson to Joseph F. Estes, 16 November 1948, RSA.
144 LR to MG, 22 November 1948, RSA.
145 Joseph F. Estes to LR, 7 March 1949, RSA.
146 Lucy Drage to LR, 29 December 1951; Lucy Drage, Inc., list of Raymer pieces on consignment, May 1953, RSA.
147 "Local Crafts in KSC Decorative Art Show," *LN-R,* undated clipping, RSA; John F. Helm, Jr. to LR, 18 November 1949, RSA.
148 Philbrook Art Center, Tulsa, OK, notice, 6 May 1944, RSA.
149 "Raymer's Work In National Show," *LN-R,* undated clipping, RSA.
150 "Raymer's Work Hung In Important Show," *LN-R,* 24 July 1947.
151 "4 Local Artists In 6-State Art Exhibit," *LN-R,* 10 February 1949
152 Mulvane Art Center, Topeka, KS, notice, n.d., RSA.
153 When Margaret Greenough sent Raymer a check for one of his ceramic vases she attached a note with the remark "wish it were 'The Three Joeys' this check was for!" Margaret Greenough to LR, 18 June 1949, RSA.

154   David E. Bernard to LR, 12 June 1950, RSA.
155   "Red Barn Artists' Works Are Being Exhibited at W.U.," *Wichita Eagle*, 25 February 1951;
          "Faculty Members Give Impressions of Raymer Art Exhibition," *Sunflower* [Municipal
          University of Wichita], 1 March 1951.
156   David E. Bernard to LR, 6 March 1951, RSA.
157   Alexander Tillotson to LR, 1 February 1955, RSA.
158   Dorothea Pellett, "Works of Lindsborg Artist Now on Exhibit," *Topeka Daily Capital*, 9
          January 1955.
159   "Mulvane Art Center Painting is Lauded in Life Magazine," *Topeka Daily Capital*, [?]
          February 1955.
160   "The First Kansas Painters Exhibit," pamphlet, June 1949, RSA; "Lindsborg Paintings in
          Painters' Exhibit," *LN-R*, 18 May 1950; "Raymer's Painting Praised in Exhibit," *LN-R*,
          28 June 1951; Robert Cooke and Vincent Campanella to LR, 4 May 1952, RSA;
          "Raymer's Painting Receives Recognition," *LN-R*, 23 July 1953.
161   "Lindsborg Art Among Approved," *Salina Journal*, 15 February 1950; John F. Helm, Jr. to
          LR, 20 March 1950, RSA.
162   John F. Helm, Jr. to LR, 14 April 1950, RSA.
163   "State Painters Featured in 7 Kansas Libraries," *Topeka Daily Capital*, 16 January 1955.
164   "$100,000 Worth of Pictures To Be Shown," *Hutchinson News-Herald*, [?] June 1949;
          "State Artist Show Works," *Hutchinson News-Herald*, 30 September 1951.
165   Captioned photograph, *Hutchinson News-Herald*, 31 January 1955.
166   Exhibition announcement card, 11 December 1955, RSA; "Four Raymer Pictures Sold,"
          Hutchinson News-Herald, 28 December 1955.
167   Second Air Capital Annual Exhibition, 13-27 February 1955, pamphlet, RSA.
168   "Faculty Members Give Impressions."
169   Pellett, "Works of Lindsborg Artist."
170   "Faculty Members Give Impressions."
171   "Two Unusual Exhibits."
172   "Faculty Members Give Impressions."
173   Pellett, "Works of Lindsborg Artist."
174   "Art in a Red Barn," np.
175   Kim Fritzemeier, "His intricate designs are gifts of art, love," *Hutchinson News*, 5 December
          1982.
176   Stolfus, "Variety characterizes." For other comments on Raymer's versatility see: Vicky, "
          'Foreign' Metalcraft Worker"; Thomas, "Ceramics Or Silver"; "Local Artists Choose";
          Rife, "Gifted, eclectic artist"; Ann Bittinger, "Artist Remembered as one of Midwest's
          finest," *Salina Journal*, 4 June 1991.
177   Greene, "Artist Achieves."
178   Ibid.
179   Peggy Greene, "For the special gift at Christmas...He shops among his talents," *Midway: the
          magazine of the Topeka Capital-Journal*, 12 December 1965, 12.
180   John P. Simoni, "Lindsborg Artist Shows Finer Scene Tradition," *Wichita Eagle-Beacon*, 23
          October 1960.
181   Thomas, "Ceramics Or Silver."
182   Simoni, "Kansans Oils."
183   The RSA collection is replete with examples.
184   Letter to LR, 8 July 1984, RSA.
185   Letter to LR, 2 August 1948, RSA.
186   Letter to LR, 14 October 1973, RSA.
187   Letter to LR, 10 September 1985, RSA.
188   Marie Flaming Rupp, "Ex Kansan Paints Old Hometown," *Wichita Eagle and Beacon
          Magazine,* undated clipping, RSA.
189   Ibid.
190   Earl Stroh, "Homage to Milford," typescript, MGP.
191   Rupp, "Ex Kansan Paints."
192   *Daisy* [Bethany College Yearbook], 1947, 29.
193   LR to MG, c. October 1948, RSA.
194   LR to MG, 12 October 1948, RSA.
195   RR to MG, [?] October 1948, RSA.
196   LR to MG, [?] October 1948, RSA.
197   LR to MG, 22 May 1949, RSA.
198   LR to MG, 28 May 1949, RSA.
199   LR to MG, 3 June 1949, RSA.
200   LR to MG, 14 July 1950, RSA.
201   LR to MG, 23 November 1948, RSA.
202   LR to MG, 22 November 1948, RSA.
203   LR to MG, 23 November 1948, RSA.
204   LR to MG, [?] October 1949, RSA.
205   LR to MG, 30 April 1949, RSA.
206   LR to MG, 7 May 1949, RSA.
207   LR to MG, 30 April 1949, RSA.
208   LR to MG, 7 May 1949; MG to LR, 5 April 1950; LR to MG, 18 November 1948, all in RSA.
209   LR to MG, 18 November 1948; LR to MG, 6 November 1949, both in RSA.
210   MG to LR, 1 May 1949, RSA.

211   LR to MG, 2 November 1948; LR to MG, 2 April 1949; LR to MG, 31 October 1949, all in RSA.
212   LR to MG, 22 November 1948, RSA.
213   LR to MG, [?] October 1949, RSA.
214   LR to MG, 9 November 1948, RSA.
215   LR to MG, 26 January 1949, RSA.
216   LR to MG, 26 May 1950, RSA.
217   MG, "Biography" [typewritten résumé], MGP.
218   Biographical notes, handwritten, n.a., n.d., MGP.
219   MG, "Biography."
220   MG to LR, 3 February 1955, RSA.
221   Ibid.
222   MG to LR, 3 August 1963; MG to LR, 5 April 1966, both in RSA.
223   MG to LR, 27 June 1955, RSA.
224   MG to LR, 4 November 1955, RSA.
225   LR to MG, 13 April 1955, RSA.
226   MG to LR, [?] 195[?], RSA.
227   MG to LR, 20 November 1955; MG to LR, 7 February 1956, both in RSA.
228   LR to MG, 26 January 1957, RSA.
229   MG to LR, 15 May 1956; LR to MG, 18 September 1956; LR to MG, 25 June 1959, all in RSA.
230   LR to MG, c. November 1957; LR to MG, 17 July 1959; MG to LR, c. August 1959, all in RSA.
231   LR to MG, 26 July 1960, RSA.
232   LR to MG, 26 August 1960, RSA.
233   For example, see the correspondence from 29 November 1960 to 9 September 1961, RSA.
234   LR to MG, 12 April 1961, RSA.
235   MG to LR, 15 February 1962, RSA.
236   LR to MG, 12 April 1961, RSA.
237   LR to MG, 23 February 1962, RSA.
238   LR to MG, 25 September 1961, RSA.
239   LR to MG, 27 July 1962, RSA.
240   W. Thetford LeViness, "Kansan's Art Wins Acclaim in Taos," [name of newspaper missing],
          25 April 1965, MGP.
241   Flo Wilks, "Milford Greer Paintings Exhibit Opens at Botts Hall Reception," [name of news-
          paper missing], 2 February 1964; "Milford Greer's First Taos Solo Show Opens At
          Gallery A May 16," [name of newspaper missing] [?] 1964; LeViness "Kansan's Art
          Wins"; Robert A. Ewing, "Milford Greer's death brings special sadness," *New Mexican,*
          9 April 1972, all in MGP.
242   "Announces Taos School of Music Plans For Fourth Summer Season," [name of newspaper
          missing], c. July 1966; "Album Shop Has New Ownership and Manager," [name of
          newspaper missing], 11 September 1966, both in MGP.
243   Nancy Stadler, "Homage Paid to Artist Milford Greer," *Moundridge Journal,* 27 April 1972.
244   LR to MG, 8 April 1956, RSA.
245   LR, handwritten document, RSA.
246   "Raymer's Work Hung In Important Show," *LN-R,* 24 July 1947; Raymer's Work in Large
          Exhibitions," *LN-R,* 18 December 1947; Eugene Kingman to LR, 31 March 1952,
          RSA; "Raymer Represented In Midwest Exhibition," *LN-R,* 1 March 1954; Pellett,
          "Works of Lindsborg Artist": "Kansas Artist In Library Show," *Rambler* [St. Benedict's
          College], 1 February 1955; Second Air Capital Annual Exhibition, 13-27 February
          1955, pamphlet, RSA.
247   Jessica Crafton to LR, 16 May 1950; Mrs. David Patterson to LR, 11 May 1954; Mrs. S.J.
          (Peggy) Donovan to RR, 12 June 1954, RSA; Pellett, "Works of Lindsborg Artist";
          Alexander Tillotson to LR, 1 February 1955, RSA.
248   Thomas, "Ceramics Or Silver."
249   Greene, "Artist Achieves." Raymer once wrote to Greer that "we went to church, and
          contrary to rule it was most rewarding to me, I actually came away with some inspi-
          ration. Unusual for me!" LR to MG, 2 November 1948, RSA.
250   Elma Byrne, "Lester Raymer Lives in World of Art," *Wichita Sunday Eagle,* 25 February 1968.
251   Jerry Bywaters to LR, 11 January 1958, RSA.
252   M.S.G. [Margaret Sandzén Greenough], "Art Gallery Notes," *LN-R,* 6 March 1958.
253   Jerry Bywaters to LR, 2 July 1958, RSA.
254   "Easter in Dallas," *Newsweek,* 7 April 1958, 62.
255   Jerry Bywaters to LR, 11 January 1958, RSA.
256   "Easter In Dallas," 62.
257   Jerry Bywaters to LR, 2 July 1958, RSA.
258   M.S.G. [Margaret Sandzén Greenough], "Art Gallery Notes," *LN-R,* 22 May 1958.
259   "Lester Raymer Wins An Award in National Art Exhibition," *LN-R,* 6 October 1960.
260   Reverend William B. Davidson to LR, 18 October 1960, RSA.
261   *Wichita Eagle-Beacon,* 14 October 1960.
262   "The new look in Religious Art," *Parade Magazine,* 11 December 1960, 27.
263   Mrs. DeBock to LR, 11 December 1960, RSA. Raymer found the letter "amusing in a way."
          LR to MG, 15 December 1960, RSA.
264   Reverend William B. Davidson to LR, 5 August 1964, RSA.
265   "Lester Raymer Wins First in Art Exhibit," *LN-R,* 24 September 1964.
266   LR to MG, 21 October 1949, RSA.
267   Wilfred Hotaling to LR, 14 November 1949, RSA.

268   LR to MG, 21 October 1949, RSA.
269   Wilfred Hotaling to LR, 14 November 1949, RSA.
270   "Local Artist's Sculptures Dedicated Last Sunday," *LN-R*, 28 May 1953; M. Moran to LR, 4 December 1953; LR to MG, 21 February 1957, both in RSA.
271   Elston Flohr to LR, 8 November 1957, RSA; M.S.G. [Margaret Sandzén Greenough], "Art Gallery Notes," *LN-R*, 27 March 1958.
272   Eugene Wukasch to LR, 9 September 1957; Elston Flohr to LR, 14 September 1957; Eugene Wukasch to LR, 30 October 1957, all in RSA.
273   Eugene Wukasch to LR, 14 October 1957, RSA.
274   Elston Flohr to LR, 8 November 1957, RSA.
275   Eugene Wukasch to LR, 12 November 1957, RSA.
276   Elston Flohr to LR, 17 December 1957; Elston Flohr to LR, 27 March 1958, both in RSA.
277   Charles Edward Stade to Reverend C.F. Wittenstrom, 6 August 1958, RSA.
278   "A 'Masterpiece' By A Local Artist for an Illinois Church," *LN-R*, 8 December 1958.
279   Janet Hart Heinecke, "The Cross is Conspicuous," *Lutheran Companion,* 26 August 1959, 6.
280   "Thanksgiving Day Dedication of St. David's," *Churchman,* November 1961, 1.
281   Reverend Henry H. Breul to LR, 17 November 1961, RSA.
282   Zula Bennington Greene, "Peggy of the Flint Hills," *Topeka Daily Capital,*, 12 November 1961.
283   "Thanksgiving Day Dedication"; Reverend Henry H. Breul to LR, 26 March 1962, RSA.
284   Lucinda S. Foster to LR, 29 August 1962, RSA.
285   "Mosaic Cross is Mounted," *Topeka Daily Capital,* 11 November 1961.
286   Malcolm Esping [obituary], *LN-R*, 5 October 1989.
287   "Fifty-Sixth Art Exhibit Being Held This Week, *LN-R*, 2 April 1953.
288   LR to MG, 25 September 1961, RSA.
289   LR to MG, 25 October 1960, RSA.
290   LR to MG, 1 August 1960, RSA.
291   "Watercolor By Raymer Projects New Park Plan," *LN-R*, 23 February 1967.
292   LR to MG, 25 September 1961, RSA.
293   LR to MG, 23 February 1962, RSA.
294   LR to MG, 22 May 1962, RSA.
295   Byrne, "Lester Raymer Lives." Although this article appeared in the winter of 1968, a letter from Byrne a day after its publication indicates that the interview occurred in the summer of 1967. Elma Byrne to LR, 26 February 1968, RSA. On Raymer's dislike of deadlines see also Becky Johnson, "Art is What He Wanted," *Bethany Messenger,* 8 November 1968.
296   Dorothy Wood, "A Good Life to Envy," *Wichita Beacon,* 13 August 1969.
297   Greene, "For the special gift."
298   Steve Russell, "Artist Makes Christmas Toys for Wife," *McPherson Sentinel,* 27 December 1969.
299   "Toys by Lester Raymer," *Kansas!,* December 1969, 10-12. This article was later translated into Yugoslavian and published in the magazine *Pregled,* as reported by Joleen Knudson, "Raymer Carries On With Unusual Tradition," *LN-R*, 18 December 1980. The Wichita Art Association exhibition was reviewed in "Display Shows Toys Made for Wife," *Wichita Eagle Beacon,* 21 June 1970.
300   Russell, "Artist Makes Christmas Toys."

301   List of Raymer exhibitions at the Birger Sandzén Memorial Gallery (1958-1993) provided by Gallery Staff, RSA.
302   LR to LS, 10 January 1978, LSPP.
303   LR to LS, 28 February 1981, LSPP.
304   "Multi-talented artist continues his work in Lindsborg," *Destination Lindsborg,* Fall & Winter, 1989-1990, 9.
305   LR to LS, 6 June 1989, LSPP.
306   Pete, Pelham, Margaret Greenough to LR and RR, 21 December 1980, RSA.
307   Novelene Ross to LR, 19 January 1990, RSA.
308   Letter to LR, 9 January 1975, RSA.
309   LR to LS, 13 April 1988, LSPP.
310   LR to LS, 5 October 1988, LSPP.
311   LR to LS, 1 December 1989, LSPP.
312   "Raymer's retrospective exhibition." On the exhibition see: Biles, "Artist who traveled"; Biles, "Student tries to explain"; Stolfus, "Variety characterizes"; Don Weddle, "In Retrospect," exhibition pamphlet, RSA; Weddle, "Lester Raymer"; Allen, "Pure Lester."
313   LR to LS, 16 August 1988, LSPP.
314   LR to LS, 5 October 1988, LSPP.
315   LR to LS, 19 March 1987, LSPP.
316   LR to LS: 8 December 1983; 19 March 1984; 25 January 1985; 28 October 1985; 10 January 1986; 16 August 1988, all in LSPP.
317   LR to LS: 3 September 1987; 31 May 1988; 16 August 1988, all in LSPP.
318   LR to LS, 20 September 1984, LSPP.
319   "Raymer honored," *LN-R*, 13 September 1984.
320   "Lindsborg's artist genius."
321   Rife, "Gifted, eclectic artist."
322   LR to LS, 23 October 1987, LSPP.
323   LR to LS, 11 October 1978, LSPP.
324   LR to LS, 22 February 1986, LSPP.
325   LR to LS, 11 October 1978, LSPP.

Six prints used by Raymer as Christmas greetings.

Reproduced as cards by the Raymer Society, 1998

326 LR to LS, 21 December, 1985, LSPP.
327 LR to LS, 10 September 1986, LSPP.
328 Lan Nelson, interview by Carla Scott and Bruce R. Kahler, handwritten notes, 9 July 1997,
        RSA.
329 LR, "Journal of trip to Europe, Ramona, Lan, and I," 29 September 1970-8 November
        1970, spiral notebook, RSA.
330 Lan Nelson, interview by Bruce R. Kahler, handwritten notes, 24 April 1998, RSA.
331 LR to LS, 13 April 1988, LSPP.
332 LR to LS, 31 May 1988, LSPP.
333 Ibid.
334 LR, handwritten document, RSA.
335 Lester Raymer [obituary], *LN-R*, 6 June 1991.

Thoughts on a Pilgrim Artist, by Diane Lincoln

Bibliography

Baldock, John. *The Elements of Christian Symbolism,* Element Books, Ltd. Shaftsbury, Great
    Britain, 1990.

Becker, Udo, ed. *The Continuum Encyclopedia of Symbols,* Continuum Publishing Company,
    New York, 1994.

Burchardt, Titus. *Mirror of the Intellect*, State University of New York Press, Albany, 1987.

Charbonneau-Lassay, Louis. *The Bestiary of Christ,* Parabola Books, New York, 1991.

Chetwynd, Tom. *Dictionary of Symbols,* Aquarian Press, London, 1993.

Chivers, Ian, Harold Osborne and Dennis Farr. *The Oxford Dictionary of Art,* Oxford
    University Press, Oxford, England, 1988.

Cirlot, J. E. A *Dictionary of Symbols,* Barnes and Noble Books, New York, 1995.

Coomaraswamy, Ananda K. *The Transformation of Nature in Art,* Dover Publications, New
    York, 1956.

Cooper, J.C. *An Illustrated Encyclopedia of Traditional Symbols,* Thames and Hudson Ltd.,
    London, 1987.

Coulter, Lane and Maurice Dixon, Jr. *New Mexican Tinwork,* University of New Mexico
    Press, Albuquerque, New Mexico, 1990.

Davies, J. G. *The New Westminster Dictionary of Liturgy and Worship,* Westminster Press,
    Philadelphia, 1986.

Ferguson, Everett. *Signs and Symbols in Christianity,* Wm. B. Eerdmans Publishing
    Company, Grand Rapids, Michigan, 1993.

Grabar, Andre. *Christian Iconography: A Study of Its Origins,* Princeton University Press,
    Princeton, New Jersey, 1980.

Green, Julien. God's Fool: *The Life and Times of Francis of Assisi,* Harper and Row
    Publishers, San Francisco, 1987.

Harvey, Van A. *A Handbook of Theological Terms,* McMillan Publishing Company, New York,
    1964.

Huizinga, J. *The Waning of the Middle Ages,* Doubleday Anchor Books, Garden City, New
    York, 1954.

Hutter, Irmgard. *Early Christian and Byzantine Art,* Universe Books, New York, 1971.

Huyghe, Rene, ed. *Larousse Encyclopedia of Byzantine and Medieval Art,* Prometheus
    Press, New York, 1968.

Jones, Alexander, ed. *The Jerusalem Bible,* Doubleday and Company, Inc., Garden City, New York, 1966.

Jorgensen, Johannes. *St. Francis of Assisi,* Doubleday and Company, Garden City, New York, 1955.

Male, Emile. *Religious Art from the Twelfth to the Eighteenth Century,* Princeton University Press, Princeton, New Jersey, 1982.

Metford, J.C.J. *Dictionary of Christian Lore and Legend,* Thames and Hudson Ltd., London, 1983.

Milburn, Robert. *Early Christian Art and Architecture*, University of California Press, Berkeley and Los Angeles, California, 1988.

Ouspensky, Leonid and Vladimir Lossky. *The Meaning of Icons,* St. Vladimir Seminary Press, Crestwood, New York, 1983.

Sendler, Egon. *The Icon: Image of the Invisible,* Oakwood Publications, Torrance, California, 1995.

Sill, Gertrude Grace. *A Handbook of Symbols in Christian Art,* Macmillan Publishing Company, New York, 1975.

Steele, Thomas J., *S.J. Santos and Saints, Ancient City Press,* Sante Fe, New Mexico, 1974.

Tuzik, Robert L. *Leaders of the Liturgical Movement,* Liturgy Training Publications, Chicago, 1990.

Walker, Barbara G. *The Woman's Dictionary of Symbols and Sacred Objects,* Castle Books, Inc., Edison, New Jersey, 1988.

Walton, Janet R. *Art and Worship: A Vital Connection,* Liturgical Press, Collegeville, Minnesota, 1991.

Watts, Alan W. *Myth and Ritual in Christianity,* Beacon Press, Boston, 1968.

White, Susan J. Art, *Architecture and Liturgical Reform,* Pueblo Publishing Company, New York, 1990.

THEMES & VARIATIONS: PAINTINGS, DRAWINGS, ILLUSTRATIONS AND PRINTS OF LESTER RAYMER, BY DON WEDDLE

FOOTNOTES

1   Dore Ashton, *Richard Lindner,* 10.

2   Lester Raymer, Interview with author, ca 1980.

3   Don Weddle, "Lester Raymer," *Southwest Art,* 64.

4   Weddle, 68.

5   It seems likely that Raymer was mindful of Picasso's dedicational opus *The Burial of Casegegemas (Evocation)*, 1901. This moving painting, heavily influenced by El Greco, could well have inspired Raymer in his need to portray his own loss.

6   Weddle, 68.

7   Lester Raymer, Interview with Dr. Greta Swenson, ca 1988.

8   Lester Raymer, Interview with Dr. Greta Swenson, ca 1988.

9   *Destination Lindsborg,* (Fall-Winter 1997-98), 2.

BIBLIOGRAPHY

Ashton, Dore. Richard Lindner. New York: Abrams, 1968.

Destination Lindsborg (Fall-Winter 1997).

Raymer, Lester. Conversation with author, circa 1980.

Raymer, Lester. Conversation with Dr. Greta Swenson, circa 1988.

Weddle, Don. "Lester Raymer." *Southwest Art,* Volume 18, Number 3 (August, 1988). 64-68.

Previous page: Coq, print, linocut, 1947.

Next page: Deer mask, papier maché and found horns. nd.

Both items in Red Barn Studio.

Untitled, oil on masonite,
1956, Red Barn Studio.

Last page, from a letter, 1986,
Raymer Society Archives.

I've scribbled on long
enough — Hope you
can read the scribble —
unfortunately I never learned
to type —
All the Best
Lou & JR